Culture and Customs
of Senegal

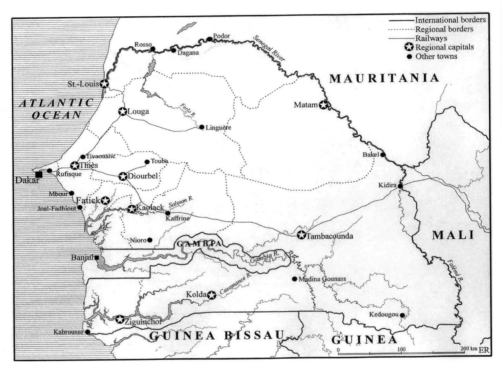

Administrative Regions.

Culture and Customs of Senegal

ERIC S. ROSS

Culture and Customs of Africa
Toyin Falola, Series Editor

GREENWOOD PRESS
Westport, Connecticut • London

Library of Congress Cataloging-in-Publication Data

Ross, Eric, 1962–
    Culture and customs of Senegal / Eric S. Ross.
        p. cm. — (Culture and customs of Africa, ISSN 1530–8367)
    Includes bibliographical references and index.
    ISBN-13: 978–0–313–34036–9 (alk. paper)
    1. Senegal—Social life and customs. 2. Senegal—Intellectual life. I. Title.
    DT549.4.R67   2008
    966.3—dc22   2008001141

British Library Cataloguing in Publication Data is available.

Library of Congress Catalog Card Number: 2008001141
ISBN: 978–0–313–34036–9
ISSN: 1530–8367

First published in 2008

Greenwood Press, 88 Post Road West, Westport, CT 06881
An imprint of Greenwood Publishing Group, Inc.
www.greenwood.com

Printed in the United States of America

The paper used in this book complies with the
Permanent Paper Standard issued by the National
Information Standards Organization (Z39.48–1984).

10 9 8 7 6 5 4 3 2 1

Contents

Series Foreword

AFRICA IS A vast continent, the second largest, after Asia. It is four times the size of the United States, excluding Alaska. It is the cradle of human civilization. A diverse continent, Africa has more than fifty countries with a population of over 700 million people who speak over 1,000 languages. Ecological and cultural differences vary from one region to another. As an old continent, Africa is one of the richest in culture and customs, and its contributions to world civilization are impressive indeed.

Africans regard culture as essential to their lives and future development. Culture embodies their philosophy, worldview, behavior patterns, arts, and institutions. The books in this series intend to capture the comprehensiveness of African culture and customs, dwelling on such important aspects as religion, worldview, literature, media, art, housing, architecture, cuisine, traditional dress, gender, marriage, family, lifestyles, social customs, music, and dance.

The uses and definitions of "culture" vary, reflecting its prestigious association with civilization and social status, its restriction to attitude and behavior, its globalization, and the debates surrounding issues of tradition, modernity, and postmodernity. The participating authors have chosen a comprehensive meaning of culture while not ignoring the alternative uses of the term.

Each volume in the series focuses on a single country, and the format is uniform. The first chapter presents a historical overview, in addition to information on geography, economy, and politics. Each volume then proceeds to examine the various aspects of culture and customs. The series highlights the mechanisms for the transmission of tradition and culture across generations: the significance of orality, traditions, kinship rites, and family property distribution; the rise of print culture; and the impact of educational institutions. The series also explores the intersections between local, regional, national, and global bases for identity and social relations. While the volumes are organized nationally, they pay attention to ethnicity and language groups and the links between Africa and the wider world.

The books in the series capture the elements of continuity and change in culture and customs. Custom is represented not as static or as a museum artifact but as a dynamic phenomenon. Furthermore, the authors recognize the current challenges to traditional wisdom, which include gender relations, the negotiation of local identities in relation to the state, the significance of struggles for power at national and local levels and their impact on cultural traditions and community-based forms of authority, and the tensions between agrarian and industrial/manufacturing/oil-based economic modes of production.

Africa is a continent of great changes, instigated mainly by Africans but also through influences from other continents. The rise of youth culture, the penetration of the global media, and the challenges to generational stability are some of the components of modern changes explored in the series. The ways in which traditional (non-Western and nonimitative) African cultural forms continue to survive and thrive—that is, how they have taken advantage of the market system to enhance their influence and reproductions—also receive attention.

Through the books in this series, readers can see their own cultures in a different perspective, understand the habits of Africans, and educate themselves about the customs and cultures of other countries and people. The hope is that the readers will come to respect the cultures of others and see them not as inferior or superior to theirs but merely as different. Africa has always been important to Europe and the United States, essentially as a source of labor, raw materials, and markets. Blacks are in Europe and the Americas as part of the African diaspora, a migration that took place primarily because of the slave trade. Recent African migrants increasingly swell their number and visibility. It is important to understand the history of the diaspora and the newer migrants as well as the roots of the culture and customs of the places from where they come. It is equally important to understand others in order to be able to interact successfully in a world that keeps shrinking. The accessible nature of the books in this series will contribute to this understanding and enhance the quality of human interaction in a new millennium.

Toyin Falola
Frances Higginbothom,
Nalle Centennial Professor in History
The University of Texas at Austin

Preface

SENEGAL IS A relatively small country, yet it is better known to North Americans and Europeans than most African countries. A number of Senegalese pop singers, Youssou N'Dour, Baaba Maal, and Ismael Lô foremost among them, are international superstars. The Senegalese writer and filmmaker Ousmane Sembène is also well known in the West. A generation ago, Senegal's founding poet-president, Léopold Sédar Senghor, was an internationally renowned intellectual. Two other Senegalese intellectuals, the scholar Cheikh Anta Diop and the mystic Ahmadou Bamba, are also well known abroad and are practically household names among African Americans. Several major U.S. cities even hold annual Ahmadou Bamba Day celebrations. Senegal is perhaps best known in the United States for the island of Gorée, which, like James Island in neighboring Gambia (made famous by Alex Haley's *Roots*), has come to symbolize the transatlantic slave trade and receives numerous U.S. visitors each year. There is thus some rationale for taking stock of contemporary Senegal and presenting its culture and customs to those who have not yet had the good fortune of coming to know the country personally.

Senegal is a formidably hospitable country, so much so that it is common to introduce it as the land of *teraanga*, or hospitality, where visitors are made to feel welcome. Yet it is also a country whose people face some of the harshest realities of the contemporary world, principally those related to grinding poverty. For instance, a common Senegalese response to the inquiry "how's it going?" is "sénégalaisement!," meaning that things are going as well as can be expected given the circumstances. The experience of any visitor to the country will thus oscillate between *teraanga* and *sénégalaisement*, and there is much to be experienced in the space between these two conditions. First of all, Senegal has a dynamic music and dance culture. These contemporary arts are in turn grounded in an ancient oral tradition that continues to thrive in modern media like novels and cinema. It is especially the public nature of Senegalese culture that distinguishes it. Senegal's arts and customs are best experienced at street level. Streets, and commercial arteries in particular, are festooned in colorful displays, while open-air dancing and music-making are part of everyday life. Even family events such as weddings, baptisms, and funerals often take place in the street, where the entire community can participate. This is also the case in religious commemorations, pilgrimages, and civic holidays, which are always loud, public, and celebratory in nature.

The task of describing the culture and customs of an entire country and its diverse people will always be beyond the capacity of a single author. This is all the truer if the author is, like I am, a foreigner to the country. I do not want to be considered an expert on Senegal. I do not speak Wolof. I know only the polite Wolof phrases necessary to cordial civility. Senegalese culture and customs have been accessible to me mainly in French or through French translation. My expertise is based on bibliographic sources, field experience, extensive travels, and observations over a 20-year-period. Moreover, while Senegal's population is more than half rural (a proportion that is steadily declining) and its contemporary culture is rooted in an ancient rural civilization, I have no direct experience with rural life. This book is thus heavily biased toward urban life and culture. As far as a general approach is concerned, I am neither an anthropologist nor an ethnographer. I am a cultural geographer (which can be likened to an anthropologist with maps). Readers of this book will thus encounter far more geography than they may ordinarily be accustomed to, but they should keep in mind that geography is simply a manner of approaching and organizing the subject matter under consideration. Far from being an exhaustive survey of Senegalese culture, this book intends to introduce the reader to as wide an inventory of artistic and cultural expressions as possible. Much of Senegalese art, music, literature, cuisine, fashion, religion, and so forth, can be accessed through the World Wide Web. Interested readers are thus encouraged to surf in search of additional or more up-to-date information.

Chronology

ca. 1350	Kingdom of Sine founded by Mandinka migrants (*gelwaar*) from Gabu.

EARLY MODERN PERIOD

1444	Portuguese navigators arrive on Senegal's coast.
ca. 1490	Koly Tenguela Ba defeats Takrur, establishes the kingdom of Futa Toro under Denyanke dynasty.
16th century	Development of Luso-African communities on the Petite Côte (Rufisque, Portudal, Joal) and Casamance.
ca. 1549	Battle of Danky. Amari Ngoone defeats Jolof Empire, unites kingdoms of Kayor and Baol. Walo, Sine, and Saloum also become fully independent kingdoms.
1621	Dutch establish factory on Gorée Island.
1633	French create first chartered company for trade in Senegal.
1651	English build Fort James near mouth of Gambia River.
1659	French establish factory of Saint Louis near mouth of Senegal River. Beginning of development of the Franco-African Métis community.
1673–1677	Tubenan (or Shurbuba) Islamic revolution in Futa Toro and Wolof kingdoms.
1677	French take Gorée from Dutch.
ca. 1690	Foundation of Islamic center of Pire by Khali Amar Fall.
1693	Establishment of Imamate of Bundu by Malik Dauda Sy.
1693–1720	Lat Sukaabe Faal unites kingdoms of Baol and Kayor.
1699	French build Fort Saint Joseph on upper Senegal River.
1716–1725	Moroccan military interventions in the Senegal valley.
ca. 1730	Foundation of Islamic center of Koki by Mukhtar Ndumbé Diop.
1758	British occupy Saint Louis.
1776	Second Islamic revolution in Futa Toro. Creation of a theocratic state by Abdul Qadir Kane.
1778	British governor of Saint Louis recognizes Charles Thévenet, a Métis, as mayor.
1779	Saint Louis reverts to French control.

1789	French Revolution. Saint Louis Métis send a list of grievances against chartered company to Paris.
1790	Islamic revolution in Futa Toro spreads to Kayor.
1791	French Republic abolishes chartered companies.
1795	Muslim clerics of Kayor are defeated.
1796	Foundation of the Lebu Republic of Ndakarou (Cape Vert) by Kayor clerics.
	Foundation of Islamic center of Mbacké by Mame Maram Mbacké.
1809	British occupy Saint Louis.
	Foundation of the Islamic center of Ndanq by the Qâdirî sheikh Bunama Kunta.
1814	Congress of Vienna abolishes slave trade. Illegal slave trading continues until 1890s.
1816	British build factory at Bathurst (Banjul), at the mouth of the Gambia River.
1817–1832	Birima Fatma Thiub unites kingdoms of Kayor and Baol.
1817	Saint Louis reverts to French control.
1819–1831	French attempt to create a cotton plantation colony in Walo.
1821	French governor recognizes Métis institutions (mayor, municipal council) in Saint Louis.
1827	Njaga Isa (the sëriñ of Koki) and Diile Fatim Thiam launch revolt against king of Walo.
1830	French defeat Diile Fatim Thiam at battle of Mbilor.
1838	French build factory at Sedhiou, in Casamance.
1840	French traders from Saint Louis establish factory in Rufisque.
1840s	Introduction of peanut cultivation.
1848	Residents of Saint Louis and Gorée recognized as French citizens. They jointly elect Durand Bartholomew Valantin, a Métis, as deputy to the National Assembly in Paris.
April 27, 1848	Definitive abolition of slavery by second French Republic.
1852	Senegal's seat in the French National Assembly is abolished.
	Al-Hajj Umar Tall launches jihad in eastern Senegal.

COLONIAL PERIOD

1855–1858	French governor Faidherbe wages war throughout the Senegal valley.
1855	Kingdom of Walo is annexed by France.
1857	Al-Hajj Omar Tall is defeated by French at siege of Medina.
	Creation of the Tirailleurs Sénégalais, an African infantry corps, to support French troops.
	French establish fort in Dakar.
1859–1865	Faidherbe invades Kayor, Baol, Sine, and Saloum and establishes "protectorates."
1861–1863	First reign of *damel* Lat Dior in Kayor.
1862	Beginning of Maba Diakhou's jihad in Badibu (Rip), Saloum, and Baol.
	Telegraph line through Kayor links Gorée to Saint Louis.
July 1867	Defeat and death of Maba Diakhou at the battle of Somb, in Sine.
1868–1869	Cholera epidemic sweeps Senegal.
1868–1883	Second reign of *damel* Lat Dior in Kayor.
1868	Beginning of Cheikhu Ahmadu Mahdiu's jihad in Jolof and Kayor.
1872	Saint Louis and Gorée recognized as French municipalities ("communes").
1875	Defeat and death of Cheikhu Ahmadu Mahdiu at the battle of Samba Sadio.
1879	The General Council, an elected consultative body for the colony, is established in Saint Louis.
1880	Rufisque obtains municipal status as French "commune."
1882	Foundation of Tiénaba by the Tijânî sheikh Amary Ndack Seck.
1883	Ndiassane established by Qâdirî sheikh Bou Kounta.
1883–1886	Saint Louis–Dakar railroad built.
1884	Seydina Limamou Laye declares himself *mahdi* in Yoff.
October 1886	Defeat and death of Lat Dior at the battle of Dekhlé. Death of *damel* Samba Laobe Fall. Kayor annexed by France.

1887	Dakar is detached from Gorée to become separate municipality.
	Foundation of Touba by Sheikh Ahmadou Bamba Mbacké.
1890s	Establishment of first Lebanese merchants in Dakar and other trading centers.
May 1890	Jolof annexed by France.
1891	Futa Toro annexed by France.
1895	Creation of the AOF, the federation of French West African colonies.
1895–1902	First exile of Sheikh Ahmadou Bamba Mbacké (to Gabon).
1902	Dakar becomes capital of AOF.
	François Carpot, a Métis lawyer from Saint Louis, is elected deputy of Senegal.
	Al-Hajj Malick Sy establishes Tijânî *zâwiya* in Tivaouane.
1903–1907	Second exile of Sheikh Ahmadou Bamba Mbacké (to Mauritania).
1906	Beginning of construction of the Dakar-Niger railroad.
1909	Galandou Diouf (representing Rufisque) becomes first African to be elected to the General Council of the colony.
1910	Al-Hajj Abdoulaye Niass establishes Tijânî *zâwiya* in Kaolack.
	Foundation of the Aurore club in Saint Louis, the first African political association.
1911–1914	Severe drought.
1912	Sheikh Ahmadou Bamba placed under house arrest in Diourbel.
1914	Blaise Diagne (from Gorée) defeats François Carpot in elections and becomes first African to sit in the National Assembly in Paris.
	Plague epidemic afflicts Dakar and the interior of the colony.
1914–1918	World War I. Thousands of Senegalese recruited to fight for France.
1918	Creation of the Faculty of Medicine in Dakar.
1919	Blaise Diagne creates the Parti Républicain Socialiste du Sénégal, the first African political party.
	First Pan-African Congress held in Paris.

1922	Boxing champion Battling Siki beats Georges Carpentier to become light heavyweight champion of the world.
1923	Completion of the Dakar-Niger railroad.
July 19, 1927	Death of Sheikh Ahmadou Bamba Mbacké.
1929	Lamine Guèye (from Saint Louis) founds the Parti Socialiste Sénégalais (PSS).
1930s	Léopold Sédar Senghor, a student in Paris, helps found negritude movement along with other black intellectuals (Léon Damas, Aimé Césaire).
1934	Defeat of Blaise Diagne. Election of Galandu Diouf to National Assembly in Paris.
1935	Establishment of Madina Gounass by Tijânî sheikh Tierno Seydou Baa.
1937	Lamine Guèye's PSS merges with the Section Française de l'Internationale Ouvrière (SFIO), the French socialist party.
	The first Senegalese trade union is created and affiliated with the French CGT (Confédération Générale des Travailleures).
1938	Creation of the Institut Français d'Afrique Noire (IFAN) in Dakar.
	First strike of railway workers in Thiès.
1939	Outbreak of World War II. Thousands of Senegalese recruited into the French army.
1940	Defeat of France by Germany. Establishment of Vichy regime. British bomb Dakar.
December 1, 1944	Mutiny of Senegalese troops stationed in Thiaroye, near Dakar.
1946	Beginning of Fourth Republic reforms, which enfranchise all Senegalese "subjects." Alliance between Lamine Guèye and Léopold Sédar Senghor.
	Creation of the Rassemblement Démocratique Africain (RDA), a pan-AOF mass political movement led by Ivory Coast's Félix Houphouët-Boigny, which mobilized for independence.
October 11, 1947 to March 19, 1948	Railway workers strike in Thiès. Strike spreads across AOF.

1948	Léopold Sédar Senghor breaks with Lamine Guèye; establishes Bloc Démocratique Sénégalais (BDS) party.
1951	Elections to the French National Assembly in Paris. Léopold Sédar Senghor defeats Lamine Guèye.
1952	Elections to the Senegalese Colonial Assembly in Saint Louis.
1954	Creation of the Mouvement Autonome Casamançais (MAC) by Assane Seck.
1956	*Loi cadre* provides for limited self-rule for all French colonies.
	Leopold Sédar Senghor leads his BDS party into a unity alliance called Bloc Populaire Sénégalais (BPS).
1957	Foundation of *Femmes de soleil* (later called *Awa*), Senegal's first women's magazine.
	Foundation of the University of Dakar.
	Majhmout Diop founds Parti Africain de l'Indépendence (PAI), a revolutionary Marxist party.
1958	AOF is dissolved. Capital of Senegal moves from Saint Louis to Dakar. Senegal votes yes in referendum on self-government within the French Union.
	Senghor's BPS and Guèye's SFIO join to form the Union Progressiste Sénégalaise (UPS).

INDEPENDENCE

April 4, 1960	Independence agreement signed in Paris. Colonies of Senegal and French Sudan to form the Federation of Mali.
June 20, 1960	Effective independence of Federation of Mali.
August 19, 1960	Federation of Mali is dissolved.
August 31, 1960	Léopold Sédar Senghor elected president of Senegal. Mamadou Dia becomes prime minister. PAI is banned.
1961	Bloc des Masses Sénégalaises (BMS) party founded by Cheikh Anta Diop.
December 1962	Constitutional crises. Mamadou Dia arrested, tried for treason, and imprisoned.
1963	Senegal is a founding member of the Organization of African Unity.
	Inauguration of Great Mosque of Touba.

March 3, 1963	Second constitution approved in referendum. Senghor reelected president unopposed. BMS is dissolved.
1964	The Front National du Sénégal (FNS) party founded by Cheikh Anta Diop.
	New family code, a mixture of the Islamic and French jurisprudences, passed into law.
	Law of national domain places all nondeeded land under the state's control, theoretically extinguishing all previous forms of rural land tenure.
1965	FNS is banned. UPS becomes sole legal party.
1965–1973	Period of severe drought. Peanut production declines. Production and export subsidies progressively reduced and abolished.
1966	Dakar hosts first World Festival of Negro Arts.
1967	Assassination of Demba Diouf, a government minister, in Thiès.
1968	Elections. Senghor reelected unopposed. High school and university students strike, followed by labor unions. Strikes put down by army.
1969	Deaths of Mahecor Diouf and Fode Ngouye, the last kings of Sine and Saloum.
	Renewed strikes by students and workers. Peasants refuse to pay debts to government agencies.
	Senegal is a founding member of the Organization of the Islamic Conference.
1970	Senegal is a founding member of the Francophonie.
February 26, 1970	Third constitution approved by referendum. Abdou Diouf appointed prime minister.
1971	Peasant debts are written off.
1972	Beginning of reform of territorial administration. Creation of "rural communities."
1974	Political liberalization begins. Amnesty of political prisoners, including Mamadou Dia. Parti Démocratique Sénégalais (PDS) founded by Abdoulaye Wade.
	The Banque Centrale des Etats d'Afrique de l'Ouest (BCEAO), responsible for the common CFA franc, moves its head office from Paris to Dakar.

1976	Constitutional reform establishes multiparty system.
	The Parti Socialiste (PS) is created to replace the UPS. Majhmout Diop restores the PAI.
1977	Cheikh Anta Diop founds the Rassemblement National Démocratique (RND), which is not recognized as a political party.
1978	Senghor reelected president.
	Senegalese troops contribute to the international military intervention in Shaba Province, Zaire.
1979	Boubacar Guèye founds the Mouvement Républicain Sénégalais (MRS) party.
December 1980	Léopold Sédar Senghor resigns from the presidency and retires from politics. Abdou Diouf becomes president. Habib Thiam appointed prime minister.
July 1981	Attempted coup in the Gambia. Senegalese forces intervene in support of Gambian president Jawara.
December 12, 1981	Senegal and the Gambia form the Confederation of Senegambia.
Spring 1982	Creation of the Mouvement des Forces Démocratiques de Casamance (MFDC), an armed movement aiming at independence for the region.
December 26, 1982	Outbreak of violence in Casamance. Beginning of armed conflict.
April 3, 1983	Moustapha Niasse replaces Habib Thiam as acting prime minister, but the post is abolished at the end of the month.
1983	Election of Abdou Diouf.
1987	Death of Cheikh Anta Diop.
1988	Abdou Diouf reelected in contested elections. State of emergency declared in Cape Vert region. High school and university students' strike causes cancellation of school year.
April 1989	Conflict along the border with Mauritania. Mauritanian nationals leave Senegal.
May 1989	Francophonie summit held in Dakar.
September 30, 1989	Confederation of Senegambia is dissolved.
1990	Creation of Dak'Art, a biennale of contemporary African art held every two years in Dakar.

September 1990	Set Setal youth movement in Dakar.
1991	First Gulf War. Senegal joins international coalition and sends troops. Ninety-one Senegalese soldiers based in Saudi Arabia die in a plane crash on their way back from pilgrimage to Mecca.
	First ceasefire in Casamance. The MFDC breaks into two rival factions.
April 8, 1991	Post of prime minister restored. Habib Thiam appointed a second time.
December 9–11, 1991	Sixth Summit of the Organization of the Islamic Conference held in Dakar.
1992–1993	Abdou Diouf serves as chairman of the Organization of African Unity.
1993	Creation of the Saint Louis Jazz Festival.
	Abdou Diouf reelected.
January 12, 1994	Devaluation of the CFA franc.
1998	Moustapha Niasse creates the Alliance des Forces Progressistes (AFP) party.
July 3, 1998	Mamadou Lamine Loum replaces Habib Thiam as prime minister.
March 19, 2000	Presidential elections. Abdoulaye Wade elected president.
April 5, 2000	Moustapha Niasse appointed prime minister.
January 7, 2001	New constitution adopted by referendum.
March 3, 2001	Moustapha Niasse resigns. Mame Madior Boye appointed prime minister.
April 29, 2001	Parliamentary elections. PDS and Sopi coalition win majority of seats.
October 2001	President Wade, along with several other prominent African heads of state, launches NEPAD (New Partnership for African Development).
December 20, 2001	Death of Léopold Sédar Senghor.
Summer 2002	Senegal's football team defeats France in opening match of World Cup.
September 26, 2002	Joola ferryboat disaster.

November 4, 2002	Idrissa Seck appointed prime minister.
2002	Senegal is a founding member of the African Union, which replaces the Organization of African Unity.
April 21, 2004	Idrissa Seck dismissed. Macky Sall appointed prime minister.
December 31, 2004	Peace deal with the MFDC brings end to armed conflict in Casamance.
July 23, 2005	Former prime minister Idrissa Seck arrested on corruption charges.
March 22, 2006	Attempted coup in the Gambia.
2007	Dakar chosen as 2007 Islamic Cultural Capital by ISESCO.
February 2007	Presidential elections. Abdoulaye Wade elected for second term.
June 2007	Legislative elections. PDS alliance wins majority of seats, but major opposition parties boycott the elections. Cheikh Hadjibou Soumare appointed prime minister.
	Death of Ousmane Sembène.
November 2007	Riots in Dakar over the decision of the municipal authorities to ban vendors from city streets.
2008	Abdoulaye Wade and president Thabo Mbeki of South Africa lead African opposition to the Economic Partnership Agreements (EPA) proposed by the European Union
March 2008	Eleventh Summit of the Organization of the Islamic Conference to be held in Dakar.
June 2008	Third World Festival of Negro Arts to be held in Dakar.

1

Introduction: The Geography and History of Senegal

SITUATING SENEGAL

SENEGAL IS A relatively small country in size and population. It is approximately 76,000 square miles in area, which is about the size of Missouri or Kansas, and it has just over 10 million inhabitants, equivalent to the state of Michigan in the United States and to Belgium in Europe.

Senegal is situated within a number of larger world regions. It is an African country, part of "Black" or "sub-Saharan" Africa. Senegal's African identity is essential to much of the country's contemporary culture and customs. Among other things, it helps explain the powerful agency of women in the public sphere and the importance of music and dance to family and public life. African essence is manifest in the country's visual arts, performing arts, and music. It is also manifest in its *orature,* that is, the oral traditions that constitute a good part of Senegal's historical memory. Moreover, the essence of African identity was theorized by Senegal's two towering twentieth-century intellectuals: Léopold Sédar Senghor and Cheikh Anta Diop. Pan-African solidarity has been a cornerstone of Senegal's foreign policy since independence. Senegal was a founding member of the Organization of African Unity in 1963 and of its successor, the African Union, established in 2002.

Senegal is part of the Muslim world. The vast majority of the Senegalese population is Muslim, and Islam has been present in Senegal since the eleventh century—that is to say, since the dawn of its recorded history. The country's oldest literary language is Arabic. Islam has influenced Senegal's culture and customs. Most of the country's national languages—Wolof, Pulaar, and Mandinka in particular—have absorbed substantial Arabic vocabulary. Senegal has produced exceptional Islamic scholars and Sufi poets, such as Sheikh Ahmadou Bamba Mbacké. Internationally, Senegal was a founding member of the Organization of the Islamic Conference, established in 1969.

Senegal is also an Atlantic country. At the westernmost tip of the Old World (consisting of Africa, Europe, and Asia), it was the first part of Black Africa to enter into direct contact with Atlantic Europe (namely, Portugal, then the Netherlands, France, and England) and to become involved in the triangular slave trade with the Americas. Gorée Island, near Dakar, has become synonymous with the slave trade and today serves as a living memorial. Transatlantic exchanges have been especially important to the history of music on both sides of the ocean and are discernable in common architectural traditions as well. In Senegal itself, the slaving economy of the sixteenth through the nineteenth centuries produced a warrior culture, designated as *ceddo*, whose *orature* celebrated heroic acts of courage, epic combat, and nobility of lineage. These *ceddo* qualities are still expressed in Senegal's national sport, wrestling.

Equally important to long-term cultural developments has been Senegal's insertion into the francophone world. The French presence in Senegal dates back to the early seventeenth century. The country was colonized by France in the nineteenth century, and French remains its official language today. Moreover, the modern Wolof language, especially the manner in which it is spoken in towns and cities, contains many French words and phrases. Much of contemporary Senegalese literature and cinema is expressed in French. French dominates the mass media, especially print, as well as public education. Most research in the humanities and social sciences, conducted in Senegal by Senegalese scholars, is published in French. Under the presidency of Senghor, who was later admitted to the prestigious Académie française, Senegal was one of the staunchest backers of the Organisation Internationale de la Francophonie, an international organization of countries whose language is French. Another former Senegalese president, Abdou Diouf, is currently serving as its secretary general.

Contemporary Senegal's African, Islamic, and French cultural foundations should not be seen as contradictory; affiliation with one of these world cultures does not cancel out the others. Rather, these perspectives and orientations overlay one another in dynamic ways, fashioning such unique phenomena as the powerful Sufi orders (often called brotherhoods), which are among the country's most important civil institutions, and a secular republican regime that accommodates much religion in the public sphere.

Closer to its borders, Senegal is part of the Sahelo-Sudanic zone, a semiarid bioclimatic region that stretches south of the Sahara Desert from the Atlantic Ocean to the Red Sea. The Sahelo-Sudanic zone is important historically for the spread of Islam in Africa and for the early emergence of states and cities in that area. The western end of the Sahelo-Sudanic zone, consisting of modern-day Senegal and Mali, is part of a north–south trans-Saharan cultural axis that stretches across Mauritania to Morocco. This avenue was important for the diffusion of Islamic scholarship generally, and of Sufism in particular. The history of this zone is exemplified by the powerful medieval empires of Ghana, Mali, and Songhay and by the famous cities of Jenne, Gao, and Timbuktu. This historic Malian (Malinke, Mandingo, or Mandinka) domain, which corresponds more or less to modern Mali, was a powerful and attractive cultural hearth during the earliest period of Senegal's history. Much of its precolonial political culture, and the vital griot tradition in particular, derived from Mali.

The far western end of this zone, open to the Atlantic, is called Senegambia. As a historical region, Senegambia includes the Senegal and Gambia river basins, which empty into the Atlantic, as well as parts of surrounding countries: the emirates of southern Mauritania, the kingdoms east of the Senegal River (western parts of modern Mali), Futa Jallon (modern Guinea), and Guinea Bissau (historical Gabu). The modern state of Senegal is central to this region. The Gambia, a former British colony, constitutes a narrow enclave within Senegal, and it isolates Senegal's Casamance region from the rest of the country. Senegal and the Gambia have close cultural and social ties, and from 1981 to 1989 they were loosely united within a political entity called the Senegambian Confederation.

THE LAND

Senegal's physical landscape is characterized by flatness and by varying degrees of aridity. The country's highest peak is in the Bassari Hills in the extreme southeast, which rises to only 1,906 feet. Most of the rest of the country consists of an immense plain less than 200 feet above sea level. This plain is subject to the tropical monsoon climate characteristic of the entire Sahelo-Sudanic zone. The rains come from the south in the hot summer months (June to October), which constitutes the agricultural growing season. The rest of the year (November to May) is mostly dry, with desiccating winds, called the *harmattan,* coming from the Sahara to the north and east. Coastal areas between the cities of Saint Louis and Dakar, on the other hand, are subject to cooler winds off the Atlantic called the *alizé.* Senegal is situated along the northern fringe of this monsoon system. Average yearly rainfall varies from over 50 inches in the wet lower Casamance region in the south to less than 10 inches in the arid northern Ferlo.

Most of central Senegal, including what is called the "Peanut Basin," is characterized by extensive dry farming. Crops are sown on fields that have been previously subjected to burning. Ashes from scrub and brush provide valuable nutrients for soils that otherwise are light, sandy, and very permeable and that receive little manure. In such light soils the hoe is preferred to the plow, and fields can be left fallow for many years between plantings. The resulting savannah landscape, typical of the Sahelo-Sudanic zone, consists of fields and pasture beneath a very light canopy of kapok trees, baobabs, and acacias, which become sparser and smaller as one travels from the humid south to the drier north. This is not a natural landscape; rather, it is the product of many centuries of agricultural and pastoral activity. Historically, various types of millet and sorghum have constituted the staple cereals, and their production dominated subsistence agriculture. Beans (*nebbe* in Wolof) were also grown along with these cereals. In the early modern era, when American plants diffused across the Atlantic, corn was added to the list of subsistence crops. In the 1840s, another American plant, the peanut, was introduced as an export cash crop.

The result of the introduction and promotion of peanut cultivation during the colonial era is the Peanut Basin. The Peanut Basin extends east from the coast, as far inland as rain-fed cultivation will allow, and south to the Gambian border. It is the agricultural heartland of modern Senegal. Yet this basin—the product of a colonial cash-crop economy with its railroads, rail towns, and port facilities—also overlays the historic heartland of the Wolof and Sereer people, namely the kingdoms of Kayor, Baol, Sine, and Saloum. These are among the oldest and most densely settled regions of the country. Villages are nucleated and spaced close together. Local traditions are deeply rooted. Even though peanut production has declined dramatically since the late 1960s, the Peanut Basin still constitutes Senegal's cultural, economic, social, and demographic heart.

In the drier interior areas of the country, such as the Ferlo east of the Peanut Basin, where rainfall is less than 15 inches per year, cattle raising is the only viable means of livelihood. The Sahel grasslands of the Ferlo, homeland of the pastoral Peul (Fulbe or Fula) ethnic group, constitute summer pasture. During the dry winter months the cattle are herded into the settled agricultural areas to the west and south, where they graze in fallow or harvested fields. The cattle are of the tropical *zebu* and *ndaama* types. The *zebu* is a very beautiful animal. Generally white, both males and females have long, graceful horns. Similar tropical breeds have a long history in Africa. They appear on Neolithic-era rock-art murals in the mountains of the Algerian Sahara as well as in the art of ancient Egypt. While the Peul raise *zebu* for meat, as other pastoral people do, they value their livestock mostly for milk. Repeated and prolonged bouts of drought since the late 1960s have severely jeopardized this pastoral way of life. The increasing desiccation of the Sahel zone may very well be a long-term process. The powerful empire of Jolof, which dominated the northern half of what is today Senegal from about 1200 to 1549 C.E., was centered in the Ferlo, an area where virtually no sedentary agriculture is possible today.

Cattle are raised in a sedentary subsistence fashion on farmsteads throughout Senegal, where they are an important source of manure for fields. This is particularly true of the densely settled Sereer lands. Sheep are also raised in Senegal. Their presence can be partly ascribed to Islamic tradition, which recommends the slaughter of a ram and the serving of lamb and mutton on certain feast days. Sheep can be raised alongside *zebu* in a pastoral-transhumant fashion or as part of traditional subsistence farming. They are invariably raised for butchery, as they produce little wool in the hot climate; wool, in any case, is not used for the weaving of cloth or furnishings such as carpets, common in other parts of the Muslim world. Goats, too, are common in Senegal, and they strongly resemble gazelles. Draft animals include mules and donkeys. The breed of donkeys most common in Senegal has fine features and markings that resemble those of zebras. Horses have traditionally been raised for use by the nobility in warfare.

In northern Senegal, along its border with Mauritania, runs the river for which the country is named. Similar to the Nile, the Senegal River runs through an area that ordinarily would be too dry for agriculture. It is the water of the river, carefully channeled through irrigated perimeters, that makes the Senegal River valley a lush agricultural zone. The valley floor (the *waalo*) is intensively cultivated, while the dry uplands on the south bank (the *jééri*) serve as pasture, for collecting firewood and for the occasional millet field. The Senegal valley is historically important, as most of Senegal's currently constituted ethnic groups—the Wolof, the Sereer, the Lebu, and the Halpulaaren—trace their origins there. Furthermore, the oldest recorded state in Senegal, the kingdom of Takrur, was located in the Senegal River valley and was the first part of the country to adopt Islam and be described in Arabic sources. The decision by French colonial authorities in the 1920s to transform the river into a border has had a negative impact on human development there. The historically central region has become peripheral to the mainstream of Senegal's economic geography, now centered in the Peanut Basin, and a bloody border conflict with Mauritania broke out there in 1989.

Southern Senegal is called the Casamance, after its own river. The Casamance is relatively isolated from the rest of the country by the Gambia and is distinctive in a number of ways. As indicated earlier, the region receives considerably more rainfall than areas farther north. The Lower Casamance, at the Atlantic end of the region, is inhabited by the Diola (or Jula) ethnic group. It is characterized by the cultivation of rice, manioc, and oil-producing palm trees. Rice cultivation in particular is essential to Diola identity. Rice paddies consist of carefully managed dikes and ditches carved out of wetland mangroves, while linear villages occupy the low ridges above. Over the past century, indigenous African strains of rice, known for their hardiness and resistance to drought, have been mostly replaced by imported strains from Asia that produce higher yields. The complex, labor-intensive landscape technologies of rice cultivation are a source of pride for the Diola, as is their history of autonomy and independence. While all people of modern Senegal have a precolonial history of statecraft, only the Diola have persistently refused centralized authority, preferring an acephalous system of independent village polities, which thrived until French colonization. More recently, the independent mindedness of the Diola, many of whom are Christians, contributed to an armed separatist movement that battled government troops on and off for 22 years (1982–2004).

Upstream from the Diola, the Middle and Upper Casamance resemble the Gambia. The region was effectively part of the empire of Mali in medieval times, and thereafter it was included within the empire of Gabu, a successor Mandinka state centered on modern-day Guinea Bissau. Malian culture has thus greatly influenced local culture, which is particularly relevant to this region's involvement in contemporary sculpture and dance. While rice cultivation and cattle raising have been historically dominant sources of livelihood in the Upper Casamance, cotton has of late become an important export crop.

As introduced earlier, Senegal's Atlantic facade is important to its historical and contemporary cultural geography. The Senegal, Saloum, Gambia, and Casamance rivers all drain into the Atlantic. Rich in fishing resources, the rivers and coast have attracted human settlement since the Paleolithic times. Fish is an important part of the Senegalese diet, and fishing, mostly "artisanal," or small scale in character, is important to the economy of all coastal communities. Nearly all of Senegal's main cities, historical and contemporary, are port cities, including Dakar, the capital. Senegal's tourism sector is beach oriented, particularly along the Petite Côte and in the Casamance. The maritime deltas at the mouths of the Senegal, Saloum, and Casamance rivers are havens for migratory birds and other wildlife and have been designated as national parks and sanctuaries.

Much of Senegal's contemporary human geography, including its transportation network and civil administrative system, is derivative of colonial-era peanut production. Like other colonies in Africa, Senegal was expected to pay for its own occupation and contribute to the economy of France. It did this by supplying industrial quantities of peanut oil for the industries of France. Consequently, the Peanut Basin's infrastructure contains the highest concentration of cities and transportation. Export of peanuts, either raw or as processed oil, was first facilitated by a rail network built between 1885 and 1932 and then by a network of paved roads following World War II. This network consolidated the importance of port cities such as Saint Louis, Rufisque, Dakar, and Kaolack as railheads, and they connected at a major inland hub, the city of Thiès. Other urban centers were created as *escales,* "landings" or rail stops, all along the railways. Civil administration, embryonic during the colonial period but reinforced following independence, was anchored in this urban network. Today, not only has peanut production declined but some of the rail lines have been shut down. Nonetheless, the human geography created by the colonial-era extraction economy lives on in the country's urban network and administrative structure.

PEOPLE AND LANGUAGES

As is the case in most sub-Saharan countries, Senegal consists of a number of diverse ethnolinguistic groups. Beyond this diversity, however, there is considerable commonality. All six of contemporary Senegal's "national" languages (Wolof, Sereer, Diola, Pulaar, Soninke, and Mandinka) belong to the Niger-Kordofanian linguistic family. This family stretches across the breadth of the continent from Senegambia to east and southern Africa, and it includes the various Bantu languages (Swahili, Zulu, Kongo, etc.) as well as Yoruba, among others. Furthermore, Senegal's various languages are grouped within the "West Atlantic" branch of Niger-Kordofanian, and though they are not mutually intelligible, they are nonetheless closely related.

Wolof is by far the most important Senegalese language, both demographically and culturally. No official statistics on the breakdown of the population by language are published, but it is generally agreed that about 50 percent of Senegalese speak Wolof as a first language (there were an estimated 3,568,060 native Wolof speakers in 2002), and an additional 20–30 percent speak it as a second language—making it the most widely spoken language. The current importance of Wolof resides in the political history of Senegal. The Wolof people were at the heart of the Jolof Empire (ca. 1200–1549) and of the subsequent independent kingdoms of Walo, Kayor, and Baol. These kingdoms controlled access to Atlantic trade with the Europeans and thus benefited more from this contact than states farther inland. Thereafter, the Wolof constituted the core African population of colonial cities such as Gorée and Saint Louis and formed the majority of the African civil service in the French colony of Senegal. Though French has remained the official language since independence, Wolof dominates national broadcast media. The process of "Wolofization" is an ongoing one. Use of the language is increasing in everyday life and in official circles. Moreover, there are distinct dialects of the language. Rural areas preserve an older, classical form of Wolof, identified as "deep" Wolof. This is the form used in the griot-based folk music, involving *xalam* playing and praise singing. On the other hand, a modern, "French-ified" form of Wolof is spoken in cities, especially among young people, and it is used in the urban *mbalax* and in the rap and pop music genres.

Closely related to Wolof is Sereer, with an estimated 1,154,760 speakers in 2002 (about 15 percent of the population). The Sereer people dominated the historic kingdoms of Sine and Saloum. They also constituted a significant proportion of Baol's population. In contrast to the Wolof states, the political culture of Saloum and Sine owed much to the empire of Mali and succes-sor Mandinka states in Gabu and the Gambia. Prior to the twelfth century it is probable that the area inhabited by the Sereer extended much farther north than it does today and "relic" Sereer communities such as the Noon (near Thiès) survive within the Wolof areas. Prior to the colonial period, the Sereer fiercely resisted attempts to convert to Islam. The kingdom of Sine, which controlled most of the Petite Côte, was exposed to Catholi-cism through the agency of Portuguese traders and the Luso-African coastal communities. The Sereer thus make up the majority of Senegal's Chris-tian population today. Léopold Sédar Senghor, Senegal's first president, was Catholic and a Sereer.

The Lebu, who inhabit the strategic Cape Vert Peninsula, constitute a subgroup of the Wolof-Sereer and speak Wolof. Though they number only about 50,000, they are the original landowners of the greater Dakar region (an agglomeration of nearly 3 million people today), a fact of considerable political and economic importance for Senegal's capital. The Lebu first se-cured their independence from the kingdom of Kayor in the 1790s, con-stituting a tiny federal republic on the peninsula under the sovereignty of a lineage of Muslim clerics, the *sërñs* of Ndakarou (the precolonial name of Dakar). Whereas all other precolonial titles and polities were abolished fol-lowing independence, the Sëriñ Ndakarou is still recognized as the leader of the Lebu by the Senegalese government. Moreover, many Lebu are members of the Layène Sufi order, another trait that reinforces their distinct regional-ethnic identity.

The second most important Senegalese ethnolinguistic group, historically and demographically, is the Halpulaaren, that is, speakers of Pulaar. All told, there are approximately 2.5 million Pulaar speakers in Senegal (nearly one-quarter of the population). What distinguishes the Halpulaaren is that there are Pulaar-speaking communities spread across the western half of the Sahelo-Sudanic zone. They form the majority of the population in Guinea's Futa Jallon region, as they do in the Masina region of Mali (the inland delta of the Niger River). Moreover, there are important Halpulaaren communities in the Hausa region of northern Nigeria and in the Adamawa Mountains of northern Cameroon. The Halpulaaren have played an important role across this zone, where they were responsible for establishing a chain of Islamic states in the eighteenth and nineteenth centuries. These include the *imamates* of Bundu (established in 1698), Futa Jallon (1725–1890), and Futa Toro (1776–1891); the Sokoto Caliphate (1804–1904); the Dina of Masina (1818–1862); Al-Hajj Omar Tall's "Toucouleur Empire" (1854–1893); and the short-lived *imamate* of Maba Diakhou in Senegal's Rip region (1862–1887).

The Halpulaaren go by a variety of designations—Fula, Fulani, Fulbe, Peul, Pulaar, and so forth—according to region, historical era, or the language of the colonizing power. In Senegal they are subdivided into two distinct groups: the Toucouleur, derived from "Takrur," and the Peul (or Peuhl), derived from "Pulaar." The Toucouleur are the sedentary inhabitants of the Senegal valley, the historic kingdoms of Takrur and Bundu. They have a long and proud history that is both documented in writing and transmitted orally. As the first Senegalese population to adopt Islam, the Toucouleur played an important role in its dissemination among the Wolof. They were the first to acquire literacy in Arabic and to use Arabic script (called an *ajami* script) to write in their own language. The kingdom of Takrur was eventually replaced by the kingdom of Futa Toro, and so the Toucouleur are also called "Foutanke," the people of the Futa. The term "Torodbe" refers more narrowly to the clerical class of Toucouleur who propagated Islam in neighboring countries. The term "Peul" refers to the traditionally pastoral Pulaar speakers who grazed their herds of cattle in the Ferlo, the semiarid expanse between the middle valley of the Senegal and the mainly Wolof-speaking Peanut Basin. This pastoral area extends southward across the Gambia River to the Fuladou, in the Upper Casamance. The Peul of this southern area have historically been sedentary, though cattle continue to be socially and culturally important. The Peul have also been more exposed to the Islam of their Mandinka neighbors than to that of their Toucouleur cousins to the north. Whether Toucouleur or Peul, the Halpulaaren have a strong sense of identity. They take great pride in their common transnational West African language and in their long attachment to Islam.

Two major Mande languages are spoken in Senegal: Soninke and Mandinka. Soninke is the mother tongue of about 200,000 people largely concentrated in the upper Senegal River valley and in Bundu. Soninke was the language of the empire of Ghana (seventh through the twelfth centuries), and its presence in eastern Senegal is thus quite ancient. A related people, the Soose, are generally believed to have been the original inhabitants of the Peanut Basin. The Sereer and the Wolof may have migrated from the Senegal valley south into the Peanut Basin in protohistorical times, over a thousand years ago. Their oral and folk traditions attribute a Soose origin to all the prehistoric structures found throughout the area, such as the megalithic circles, the tumuli, and the giant pit wells.

The Mandinka (also Mandingo, Malinke, Manding) are more numerous than the Soninke, with about 600,000 native speakers. Mandinka was the principal language of the empire of Mali (thirteenth through the fifteenth centuries), and the current distribution of Mandinka speakers in Senegambia—in the upper Gambia River basin, in central Casamance, and in Guinea Bissau—is the result of that empire's expansion into the area. Much more recently, Bambara speakers (Bambara is another Mande language, closely related to Mandinka) from present-day Mali settled in Senegal. They were employed by the French for the construction of the Dakar-Niger railroad (1906–1923). Small Bambara communities formed at rail stops all along the line, including in the city of Thiès, the main rail hub. Both Soninke and Mandinka have a strong oral tradition and thus a strong sense of their history. Though they are Muslims today, the Mandinka still value their pre-Islamic traditions of epic orature, music, dance, and masquerades.

The ethnonym Diola (or Jula) designates a group of closely related people—the Balant, the Baïnouk, the Manjak, and the Diola proper—who inhabit the lower Casamance region around Ziguinchor. They number about 350,000 (or 3.5% of Senegal's population) and are distinguished not just by language (members of the sub-Guinean linguistic group) but by history, lifestyle (the rice production described earlier), and religion. Before French colonization, the Diola constituted acephalous societies, meaning that they did not organize themselves into kingdoms or states, but rather they structured themselves as networks of autonomous villages, lineages, and spiritual fraternities. They suffered more than most other Senegalese ethnic groups from the slave raiding of the seventeenth and eighteenth centuries, and their reluctance to form states may well have been a social response to this destructive activity. Though the Diola were in close contact with Portuguese Catholicism in the fifteenth century, they only began adopting Christianity during the French colonial period. Today, like the Sereer, they are mostly Catholic. A Catholic priest, Father Augustin Diamacoune, led the ethnically based armed separatist insurrection in the Lower Casamance during the 1980s and 1990s.

ETHNICITY, NOT TRIBE

The reader may be aware at this point that the term "tribe" has not been used in the earlier descriptions of Senegal's people. Unlike Somalia, for instance, or most of the Arab countries to its north, Senegal has never been a tribal society. A tribe is a specific form of sociopolitical organization where authority is exercised through segmentary lineages that recognize a common filiation. Historically, tribal societies have often thrived outside state structures. What distinguishes one tribe from another in such societies is not language or religion but genealogical filiation—whether imagined or real. All the tribes of neighboring Mauritania, for example, the Bou Sbaa, the Tekna, and the Idou-l Hadj, are Muslim and speak Arabic. At no time in Senegal's history have Senegalese societies been tribal. Rather, like most other West African societies, they have been structured by caste. A caste is a social group defined in terms of inherited professional or spiritual qualities. Wolof members of the woodworking caste, for example, have much in common with their Toucouleur counterparts. All go by the family name Laobe, and they may intermarry. On the other hand, according to tradition, a Wolof woodworker would not be able to marry someone from the Wolof peasantry or nobility. The term "tribe" is entirely inappropriate to designate such a social structure. Though this term is commonly used in media reporting about sub-Saharan Africa (as in "tribal conflict"), what is really being designated are ethnic or ethnolinguistic groups.

No discussion of Senegal's people would be complete without mention of historically and currently important minority groups. Historically, one of the most interesting cultural groups in Senegal was the Métis, descendants of white European traders and African wives and concubines. The oldest such communities thrived along the Petite Côte in places like Rufisque, Portudal, and Joal, where the Portuguese of the Cape Verde Islands traded. These Luso-Africans, or "Lançados," maintained a Catholic identity, which distinguished them from other African traders. A French-speaking Métis community, also Catholic, emerged in the seventeenth century in the European-controlled island cities of Gorée and Saint Louis. Women were especially important members of the Métis community. They ran businesses, owned ships, and commanded male employees. Known as *siñares* (or "signares," from the Portuguese *siñora*), these women were also famous for the art of hospitality, cultivated entertainment, fine dining, fashion, and urbane demeanor. Situated very much as middlemen between the Euro-Atlantic trade and the interior hinterland, the Métis thrived until the official colonization of Senegal in the late nineteenth century. Thereafter, their political and economic importance deteriorated steadily.

Another historically and culturally important group was the Moors of present-day Mauritania. These Arabic-speaking individuals call themselves "Bîdân," or "White." In Wolof they are called "Naar." Individually and in small communities, the Moors have been present in Senegal for many centuries, and their main impact has been on the propagation of Islam and Arabic literacy. Up until the mid-nineteenth century, Moorish religious scholars and Sufi sheikhs were greatly solicited by elite groups within Wolof society. The emergence of powerful Sufi orders in Senegal in the twentieth century, however, has reversed the relationship: Senegalese Sufi sheikhs now increasingly tour Mauritania. Modern Mauritania is much poorer than neighboring Senegal. Tens of thousands of Mauritanians live in Senegal, where they work in the small retail sector or as small-time traders, and they send remittances back home. The 1989 border conflict between the two countries had a devastating impact on Mauritanians living in Senegal, as it did on Senegalese citizens and Wolof and Pulaar speakers living in Mauritania. Since then, however, the fabric of interethnic relations has been largely repaired.

The Lebanese constitute another important group within Senegal. "Syrians" from what is now Lebanon began arriving in Dakar in the 1890s when it was a booming commercial center. The Lebanese, a mix of Christians, Sunnis, and Shi'is, have been active in the import-export, wholesale, and large-scale retail sectors ever since. Based largely in downtown Dakar, Lebanese businesses can also be found in towns and cities throughout the country.

More recently still, Senegal opened its doors to immigrants and refugees from neighboring Guinea and Cape Verde. Under the presidency of Sékou Toure (1958–1984), Guinea was an authoritarian one-party state. Opposition figures, as well as many ordinary Guineans, found refuge in Senegal, and in Dakar in particular. Economic migrants from the Cape Verde Islands arrived in Dakar around the same time. Significant to any discussion of contemporary Senegalese society and culture is President Senghor's address of the citizens of the country in the 1970s: "Sénégalais, Sénégalaises, and foreigners living among us"—an indication of the positive attitude toward multiculturalism and diversity that generally permeates Senegalese society.

France, the former colonial power, still has a strong presence in Senegal. Approximately 20,000 French citizens live in the country, mostly in Dakar, where they work for banks, multinational corporations, major hotels, consultancy firms, international organizations, non-governmental organizations (NGOs), and research centers. Moreover, France maintains a military base in Senegal, next to Dakar's international airport. French is the only official language of the country, and it is the language of Parliament, the civil service, the courts of law, business, and public education. The other "national" languages discussed earlier, written in Latin script, are used in the media but only

French has official status. French culture, language, and the legacy of French colonization are thus hugely important to Senegal's own national culture.

However, the French language, though dominant today, is not completely hegemonic. Literary Arabic is still used in Senegal, as many Senegalese have been educated in that language. Arabic was the first, and for a long time the only, literary language in the country. A corollary to the propagation of Islam was literacy in Arabic because of the centrality of the Koran to Muslim life generally and because of the importance of legal texts and authenticated traditions in particular. Arabic is used as a lingua franca, orally and for written correspondence, by Muslims across Africa, whatever their native tongue might be. Senegal itself has a tradition of authorship in Arabic, meaning that Senegalese mystics, poets, and historians have written in Arabic, and some contemporary Senegalese intellectuals prefer to publish in that language today. Furthermore, while all of Senegal's national languages are written in Latin script, some, such as Pulaar and Wolof, are sometimes also written in an Arabic script; Wolof written in Arabic script is called "Wolofal." Within the Mouride Sufi order especially, Wolofal is preferred to "Latin" Wolof not just for religious uses but for such profane things as billboards and storefront signs. In this case, use of Wolofal is a mark of attachment to an Islamic identity and of rejection of the colonial heritage.

HISTORY

Senegal has been inhabited for hundreds of thousands of years, long before the creation of the oral traditions and written records relied on by historians. Much of what we know about prehistoric Senegal comes from archeology. Yet, though there is a wealth of material vestiges across Senegal, archeology has yet to deliver a complete picture of prehistoric processes.

Both the Cape Vert Peninsula and the upper Senegal River basin have yielded a range of early Paleolithic tools, namely, stone hand axes of the Acheulean era (ca. 150,000 to 50,000 B.C.E.). Subsequently, there seems to have been continuous human activity until the flowering of a number of cultures, characterized by distinctive stone tools, during the Neolithic era (ca. 5000 B.C.E. to 400 C.E.).

The protohistoric period corresponds to the late Neolithic and the Iron Age (fourth century B.C.E. to eighth century C.E.). Coastal areas, and the maritime deltas of the Casamance, Sine-Saloum, and Senegal rivers in particular, were home to fishing communities. These communities were responsible for the innumerable seashell middens, which today rise five or six feet above the tidal flats and consist of piles of discarded seashells, the refuse of centuries of shellfish consumption. Inland, a megalithic culture characterized by alignments of dressed stones flourished in the Gambia and eastern Saloum regions. This culture may have been associated with a contemporaneous tumulus culture. Earthen tumuli, called *mbanar* in Wolof and *podom* in Sereer, are found across Saloum, Sine, eastern Baol and Kayor, Jolof, and as far north as Walo. Both the megaliths and the tumuli seem to have been associated with elite burial, an indication of social stratification. Archeological investigations have unearthed pewter jewelry, iron harness fittings and spearheads, and much pottery. Local oral traditions in these areas attribute these mounds and stone circles to the "Soose," a people considered by the Sereer and the Wolof to be the original inhabitants of the land. The archeological evidence clearly indicates that Senegal was a settled land in protohistoric times, meaning that people lived in villages and pursued agriculture, animal husbandry, and fishing as means of livelihood. The existence of tumuli and megaliths in some regions indicates that social elites were able to accumulate wealth and mobilize significant manpower. These trends were strengthened with the introduction of iron around the end of the fourth century C.E.

Evidence of extensive iron smelting, along with copper, pewter, and gold working, was found in the Senegal River valley, in Bundu, in the highlands of the upper Senegal and Gambia River basins, and across central Casamance. As elsewhere in sub-Saharan Africa, iron smelting and the use of iron tools heralded a major cultural shift characterized by increased social stratification and the emergence of the first states. The kingdom of Takrur, in the Senegal River valley (today's Futa Toro), is the first historically attested state in what is today Senegal. Though Takrur is first mentioned in the work of Arab geographer Al-Bakri in 1068, analysis of the orature of Futa Toro and of the density of ancient settlements in that part of the valley indicates that a state whose elite was linked to iron working existed many centuries earlier. In this regard, Takrur is similar to two other early Sahelo-Sudanic states farther east: Ghana and Gao. These iron-working states were already in existence when trans-Saharan trade with North Africa became important in the ninth century. The Arab authors who wrote about these trade routes mention a number of trading cities on the Nile (the Senegal and Niger rivers are invariably called the Nile in these medieval texts, though the three river systems are in fact quite distinct), such as Barisa, Silla, and Takrur. Furthermore, Takrur is mentioned as a city, not a state, but these texts often conflate the names of cities, states, and rulers.

By the ninth century it was clear that one of the Sahelo-Sudanic states, Ghana, had become an empire, attempting to exert power over its neighbors and to monopolize the lucrative trans-Saharan trade. In all likelihood, the kingdom of Takrur remained independent of the empire of Ghana and competed with it for access to international trade, particularly the gold trade.

The same Arabic-language sources mentioned earlier also report that War Jaabi, the king of Takrur, was the first sub-Saharan monarch to convert to Islam, having done so before the military expansion of the Almoravids in the second half of the eleventh century. The Almoravids were a Berber tribal confederacy from the Adrar region of modern-day Mauritania. Beginning in 1050 they embarked upon a series of religiously inspired military campaigns that eventually earned them a trans-Saharan empire stretching from the border of Takrur in the south to Spain's Ebro River in the north. Takrur was not necessarily absorbed into this empire, and its Muslim king may have even formed an alliance with it against neighboring Ghana.

It is not clear what the population of Takrur consisted of at that time. Most likely it was heterogeneous, as the traditions of the current Toucouleur, Sereer, Lebu, and Wolof populations all trace their origins to the Senegal valley during this period. Also, the adoption of Islam by the king and other members of the nobility does not mean that Islam became the religion of state. Statecraft and public law continued to be conducted according to tradition, and most inhabitants of Takrur continued to adhere to traditional beliefs. Nonetheless, due to Takrur's trans-Saharan links with the Muslim world, a class of Muslim scholars, called Torodo or Torodbe, began to form there. They would eventually be instrumental in spreading Islam in Wolof-speaking countries farther south.

Political conditions in the western part of the Sahelo-Sudanic zone changed in the thirteenth century. While Takrur had survived the expansion and collapse of Almoravid power, a new state to the south, Jolof, emerged to challenge it. The epic and legendary founding of Jolof by a prince named Njajaan Njaay (also spelled Ndiadiane Ndiaye) is at the origin of the Wolof sense of identity. It appears from the relevant orature that the Jolof state was first established in Walo, the region at the lower end of the Senegal River, but that it rapidly expanded to include most of modern-day Senegal, as far south as the Gambia River, and that it held Kayor, Baol, Sine, Saloum, and even parts of Takrur as tributary provinces. Prior to the consolidation of Jolof as an empire, there had been no central political organization in most of these areas. Power had been exercised locally by *lamans,* or "landlords." The *lamans* did not so much own land as control access to it and derive revenue from the peasants who farmed it. They constituted a local landed aristocracy, and they continued to administer affairs in their small *lamanates* even after the imposition of a centralized form of monarchic rule by the *burba* (king) of Jolof. It would also seems that expert use of cavalry was a key factor in the rapid rise of the Jolof Empire. There is, however, no consensus on the date of its establishment. Some historians argue that it may have occurred as early as 1200, while others opt for a later date, ca. 1300.

Shortly after Jolof replaced Takrur as the main state in Senegambia, it was confronted by an even more powerful empire, Mali. Mali was an ancient Mandinka kingdom centered in the upper Niger River basin on the border of present-day Mali and Guinea. As in the case of Jolof, a legendary hero named Sunjata (Soundiata) Keita is credited in the orature for galvanizing his people and launching them on the path of empire building. By 1240 Mali had annexed the remnants of Ghana to the north and had initiated westward expansion into Senegambia. The Gambia and Casamance river basins were conquered by General Tirimaxan (Tirimakhan) Traore, whose heroic exploits are lauded in the orature. Mandinka farmers and traders settled in these areas in his wake. These western provinces were fully integrated into the Malian empire, and the Mandinka language and political culture survived long after the fall of the empire. Moreover, these provinces were important because they permitted access to the Atlantic Ocean and its coastal and riverine trading networks. Cola nuts, cotton cloth, and iron ingots constituted the main items of trade. This coastal navigation may have even heralded a policy of oceanic exploration; according to the Egyptian chronicler Al-Umari (ca. 1345), the Malian emperor (called the *mansa*) Abu Bakary II sent two large fleets of dugouts westward across the Atlantic at the beginning of the fourteenth century. While Mali administered the Gambian and Casamance provinces directly, Takrur and the Jolof Empire were incorporated as tributary states. Ironically, it was at this time that "Takrur" came to be used in the Muslim Middle East as a designation for Mali itself. When Mansa Kankan Musa (reigned 1312–1332) made his famous pilgrimage to Mecca, he insisted that he was not the sultan of Takrur but that Takrur was one of his provinces. Notwithstanding this disclaimer, "Takrur" continued to be used in the Middle East until the nineteenth century to designate Muslim West Africa generally.

When Mali's imperial reach declined in the mid-fifteenth century, the western Mandinka areas of Casamance and the Gambia consolidated themselves into a new entity, the empire of Gabu (sometimes spelled Kabu). Furthermore, a caste of Mandinka aristocrat-warriors, called the *gelwaar,* settled among the Sereer and established the political foundations of the kingdom of Sine. Meanwhile, the empire of Jolof reasserted its hegemony everywhere else north of the Gambia River. Portuguese navigators encountered this political situation when they first arrived off Senegal's Atlantic coast in 1444.

The opening up of Senegambia to Atlantic trade with Europe and the Americas marks a significant moment in its history, as this had a lasting impact on its societies and states. At first, the Portuguese were intent on accessing West Africa's gold production. Since the ninth century, and perhaps even earlier, gold from Bure and Bambuk had been traded across the Sahara and had enriched mostly the Muslim states of the Mediterranean. The Portuguese managed to tap into the gold trade by sailing up the Gambia River and trading at the mouths of rivers along the Guinea coast. Other commodities were also traded: ivory, spices and nuts, skins and leather, and, most importantly, slaves. The Portuguese used the Cape Verde Islands, which are situated in the Atlantic 500 miles west of Senegal, as a rear base from which they could securely trade with the continent. Trade on Senegal's coasts was conducted by communities of Afro-Portuguese (or Luso-African) "Lançados," the descendants of Portuguese traders and African women. Lançado communities thrived in Rufisque, Portudal, and Joal and at the mouths of rivers farther south by the middle of the sixteenth century. It should be noted here that these trading posts were not Portuguese colonies. They remained under African sovereignty. Europeans and Luso-Africans conducted business in these places, but they had to pay dues and duties to African kings.

In the interior of Senegambia, the opening up of the Atlantic coincided with a major geopolitical shift. First there was the migration of Halpulaaren across the length and breadth of the country. Under the leadership of yet another epic hero, Koly Tenguela Ba, cattle-rearing Pulaar speakers (Fulbe or Fulani) emerged from Futa Jallon (present-day Guinea), swept through the central Casamance, crossed the Gambia River, and devastated the heart of the Jolof Empire before seizing Takrur. The kingdom of Takrur was definitively defeated. In its place, the Fulbe established a new kingdom, Futa Toro, under the Muslim Denyanke dynasty. These events probably occurred in the last decade of the fifteenth century. While Takrur succumbed immediately to the Fulbe onslaught, the demise of the empire of Jolof was slower.

The Jolof Empire collapsed when its western provinces revolted against imperial rule and refused to pay the customary tribute. These coastal provinces, Walo and Kayor especially, were better situated than Jolof proper with regard to Atlantic trade. They benefited more directly from the resources this trade procured; thus they were able to overthrow the rule of Jolof. At the battle of Danky (1549) a young prince of Kayor, Amari Ngoone Sobel Fall, defeated the army of the *burba* of Jolof. He became *damel* (king) of an independent Kayor, as well as *teeñ* (king) of the neighboring kingdom of Baol. Such sovereign unions of Kayor and Baol under a single *damel-teeñ* occurred on several occasions in subsequent centuries, but they were always short lived. The loss of Kayor and Baol rapidly led to Walo, Sine, and Saloum declaring their independence from Jolof. The mainstream of Senegal's history had definitely shifted west, to what is now called the Peanut Basin. A rump kingdom of Jolof, under a diminished *burba,* nonetheless maintained itself in the relative isolation of the Ferlo until the French imposed colonial rule in 1890.

The newly independent kingdoms of Walo, Kayor, Baol, Sine, and Saloum were hybrid political structures. The *lamanate* system of local landed nobility continued to structure power relations. Great noble families, called *garmi,* competed for power at court, and they relied heavily on the *lamans* for support. They also relied increasingly on a caste of slave-soldiers called the *ceddo.* In the majority Sereer kingdoms of Sine and Saloum, a warrior-aristocracy of ancient Mandinka extraction, the *gelwaar,* monopolized power. These political systems were highly unstable, and there was no agreed-upon succession to the throne. Accession to power depended on both matrilineal and patrilineal kinship, as well as on the support of the warrior castes and the resources to pay for it. As a result, civil war during succession disputes was the norm, and even established kings had to constantly contend with usurpers and the intervention of neighboring kings. Civil war in one state often spilled over into others.

Moreover, instability and insecurity were further fueled by the slave-trading economy. Beginning in the seventeenth century, the diffuse Portuguese trading network was replaced by "chartered" Dutch, English, and French trading companies. These companies created permanent, more or less fortified trading posts on strategically situated islets—the Dutch on Gorée Island off the Cape Vert Peninsula; the English on James Island, at the mouth of the Gambia River; and the French at Saint Louis, on the Senegal River just upstream from its mouth. Because these European states were often at war with one another, the Senegambian trading posts changed hands many times. In the end, following the Napoleonic Wars, Gorée and Saint Louis were definitively allocated to France, while Great Britain retained a monopoly on the Gambia. Regardless of transfers of sovereignty, the slave trade continued to grow throughout the eighteenth century, and to affect the social and political development of all Senegambian states. International conflict and internecine strife became ends in themselves, the means of obtaining captives for sale rather than the means to some political outcome. The warrior orders, the *ceddo* of Wolof kingdoms and their equivalents elsewhere, rose to positions of power at the expense of the landed nobility. Certain states, such as the Gabu Empire, dominated by the *gelwaar* and enjoying advantageous access to European-manufactured firearms, specialized in the procurement of slaves. It has been estimated that anywhere between 200,000 and 500,000 slaves were exported from Senegambia in the course of the seventeenth and eighteenth centuries. The true scale of the demographic disruption this represents becomes clear when one considers that the population of the entire region was probably a little over a million at the time.

The destructive effects of the slave trade were felt in every society by every community. The institution of slavery had long been entrenched in social,

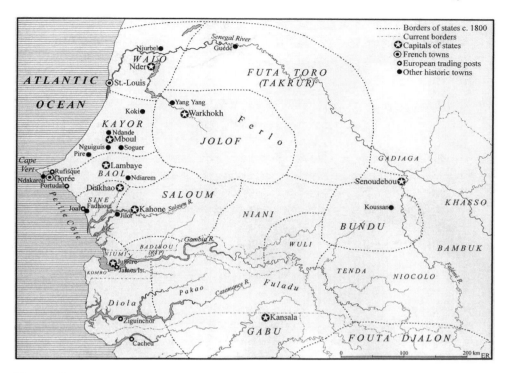

Historic States.

economic, and political relations in Senegambia. Yet the sheer quantity of slaves demanded by the plantation system in the Americas, and the perpetual nature of the violence necessary to procure these slaves in Africa, was unprecedented. When the transatlantic trade was progressively shut down by the great European powers in the first half of the nineteenth century, political elites in various Senegambian states had difficulty adapting to the new economic context, a situation that only aggravated these states' endemic political instability.

As a consequence, Senegambia experienced a series of Islamic revolutions during this period. The first, called the Shurbuba or Tubenan Revolution, erupted in Futa Toro in 1673 and spread rapidly through Jolof and Kayor. In Kayor, Muslim clerics successfully overthrew the king, but the traditional aristocracy, supplied with firearms by the French in Saint Louis, crushed the rebellion and reasserted their control of the state. The remnants of this revolution eventually set up an Islamic state, called an *imamate,* in Bundu in 1693. In 1776 Futa Toro experienced a second Islamic revolution. The *torodbe* clerics succeeded in overthrowing the Denyanke regime in Futa Toro, but their colleagues in Kayor failed in their attempt to do likewise. After their defeat at the hands of royalists in 1795, some of the Kayor clerics found refuge among the Lebu on the Cape Vert Peninsula, where they helped establish the independent state of the Lebu Republic. Similar Islamic revolts and rebellions erupted throughout Senegambia in 1827–1830, 1852–1857, 1862–1867, 1868–1875, and 1887–1888.

The two main grievances of the Muslim clerics vis-à-vis the monarchic systems they wanted to overthrow were the issues of slavery, or the conditions under which Muslims were being enslaved and sold to Christians, and taxation, or the illegitimate manner in which taxes were being extorted from peasants by *lamans* and *ceddo*. Though these Islamic revolutions met with varying degrees of success initially, they were all eventually defeated by a combination of French-supplied firepower and powerful French trading interests. Even in cases where the clerics were completely successful in overthrowing the regimes, such as in Bundu and Futa Toro, they failed to set up substantially better regimes. Instability and civil war continued to plague these states, and they continued to be fatally enmeshed in the destructive slaving economy.

Saint Louis and Gorée were the two most important trading towns on the Atlantic coast. Theoretically, they were administered by a French-appointed governor in Saint Louis who represented the interests of the officially chartered company. Such administration was practically thin on the ground. Governors rarely served more than a two-year term, and they were given little logistical or financial support from the parent company. Moreover, both Gorée and Saint Louis were frequently occupied by English forces, which disrupted attempts at long-term planning. Consequently, it was the Métis trading elite of these towns who increasingly took charge of local affairs. The Métis were the descendants of French traders and African women. Even in relatively healthy coastal locations such as Gorée and Saint Louis, Europeans survived only short periods of time in the face of infectious diseases and fevers of all kinds. During their short stints, such traders would enter into "country marriages" with African women, often of high social status. Upon the deaths of the European husbands, or their return to France, the African wives would take care of business. Moreover, the offspring of these marriages would inherit the family business. These Métis businesses usually consisted of "up-country" trading with the interior, the transoceanic shipping being firmly in the control of the chartered company and its agents. The power and influence of the Métis business class, many of whose members were women, found political expression. During the period of British rule in Saint Louis (1758–1779), the Métis began selecting one of their own to serve as mayor and to represent their interests before the governor. In 1789, when news of the revolution in France reached Saint Louis, French and Métis traders, who considered themselves part of the French nation, sent a petition of their grievances against the chartered company to the

National Assembly in Paris. The company's charter was effectively revoked in 1791, opening up trade to greater competition.

Chartered companies were not the only thing the revolutionaries in Paris abolished. In 1794 they also abolished slavery in all territories under French jurisdiction. The business milieu in Saint Louis and Gorée, however, refused to adopt or implement this provision. Slavery continued to legally exist there until its definitive abolition in 1848, and the practice continued covertly long afterward. Nonetheless, by the time of the Congress of Vienna (1814–1815) and the abolition of the international trade in slaves, the writing was on the wall: the slaving economy was going to end, and new articles of trade needed to be found. The French colonial authorities definitively regained control of the colony from the British in 1817 and attempted to institute a slave-based cotton plantation system in the kingdom of Walo, contiguous to Saint Louis, but that attempt failed. The Métis traders, for their part, invested in the gum trade. Gum arabic is a resin produced by acacia trees. It had many uses in early industrial manufacturing as well as in food processing. The gum was harvested from the acacia forests of the Sahel zone, which stretched north of the Senegal River valley eastward toward the Niger. The gum trade served as a temporary stopgap measure to cushion the decline in slave trading. The future of the colony lay elsewhere, with peanuts.

The heroic death of Lat Dior Diop, the enigmatic and youthful *damel* of Kayor, at the battle of Dekhlé in 1886 symbolically marked the end of the old regime and the culmination of colonial conquest. By 1891, the entire territory of modern Senegal had been brought under French control, the Saint Louis–Dakar railroad was operational, and peanut production was booming. At first the colonial regime adopted an indirect approach to rule. The old kingdoms were dismembered into their constituent provinces, called cantons. Local *lamans,* compliant *ceddo,* and young French-educated nobles were designated as their chiefs. As long as there was no armed opposition, and so long as taxes were collected (a key element in promoting peanut production as a cash crop for export), rural areas were left to the devises of these French-appointed "traditional" chiefs. The popular legitimacy of these local elites, however, was jeopardized by their subservient role within the colonial system. This lack of legitimacy became acute during the two world wars, when the canton chiefs were obliged to fill quotas of recruits for the French army (96,000 Senegalese men were recruited during World War I), a very unpopular activity.

In rural areas, the social vacuum caused by the demise of the old elites was filled by a new social elite, the sheikhs of the various Sufi orders. The Muslim Sufi orders (often called brotherhoods), which included the Qadiriyya, various branches of the Tijaniyya, the Mourides, and the Layènes, coalesced around a number of charismatic Muslim clerics, scholars, and mystics. To varying degrees, these orders promoted a spiritual revival of rural society. They used the emerging peanut cash-crop economy to realign peasant life. Beyond simply promoting proper Islamic conduct (prayer, fasting, righteous and upright conduct), the sheikhs stressed solidarity, self-reliance, and social responsibility based on a productive life. In the process, they built up mass movements numbering hundreds of thousands of members. At first the colonial authorities were wary of, and at times hostile to, these Sufi movements. Sheikh Ahmadou Bamba, founder of the Mouride order, was repeatedly exiled and held under house arrest, while Seydina Limamou Laye, founder of the Layène order, was briefly imprisoned. However, the authorities eventually realized that the Sufi institutions were far more influential than their own canton chiefs. A mutually beneficial accommodation was thus reached between the authorities and the sheikhs: the authorities left rural populations alone, and the Sufi orders ensured the continued expansion of peanut production. In many cases the sheikhs were granted preferential access to frontier agricultural lands.

Social developments were different in the Four Communes: Saint Louis, Gorée, Rufisque, and Dakar. These cities had the status of French municipalities, and most of their male inhabitants were fully French citizens. They elected representatives to the General Council in Saint Louis (a purely consultative body for the colony), as well as a deputy to represent them in the National Assembly in Paris. Moreover, Senegal came to occupy a commanding position in the French Empire, which stimulated growth in these cities. In 1895 all of France's West African colonies were federated within a new administrative structure, the Afrique Occidentale Française (AOF). In 1902 Dakar became the capital of this colonial federation, while Saint Louis remained the joint capital of the colonies of Senegal and newly conquered Mauritania. Dakar was already a strategic port for the French fleet and the main railhead for much of the federation, a role enhanced by the completion of the Dakar-Niger railway in 1923. Furthermore, Dakar attracted the highest-level administrative, educational, and health institutions.

Modern forms of association thrived in the Four Communes. Newspapers flourished, as did political parties and, eventually, trade unions. While the Métis lost much of their economic influence to the large Bordeaux-based trading companies that had invested in Senegal, they remained important in the liberal professions and in the burgeoning civil service, and they dominated the colony's political life until the eve of World War I. Africans, mostly Wolof speakers from the Peanut Basin, became politically active in the cities, where they constituted a majority of the population and the electorate. In 1909 Galadou Diouf became the first African to be elected to the colony's

General Council, and in 1914 Blaise Diagne was elected to represent the Four Communes in Paris. He was the first African to hold that post.

World War II further stimulated the forces of social modernization in Senegal and accelerated the nationalist and emancipatory processes that would lead to independence. Senegalese students and intellectuals in Paris had already initiated a pan-African cultural awakening akin to the Harlem Renaissance. They, as well as the tens of thousands of African troops recruited into the French army, experienced Nazism and the Vichy regime firsthand. African troops played a major role in the liberation of France, with the promise of a more equitable political regime after the war. It was not long before these raised expectations manifested themselves. The war was not even over when African troops stationed at Thiaroye, outside Dakar, protested against their poor living conditions. Their mutiny was violently suppressed. Shortly thereafter, from 1947 to 1948, the French West African railway workers union, led by the Senegalese affiliate, went on strike for better working conditions. Consequently, and in fulfillment of its wartime pledges, the French government began enacting a series of reforms aimed at extending political rights in the colonies. This culminated in 1956 with the *loi cadre,* which granted universal suffrage to all former "subjects" and extended the scope of civil liberties and democratic institutions to all colonial territories. Henceforth, every Senegalese adult became a voting citizen.

Senegalese political parties, often affiliated with major French parties, were obliged to reorient their policies. Electoral politics was no longer confined to the Four Communes, where leftist, socialist, and communist tendencies dominated. The much larger rural electorate was deeply religious and socially and intellectually dominated by the sheikhs of the Sufi orders. It is in this context that Léopold Sédar Senghor emerged as Senegal's most able political leader. Already famous as a poet and public intellectual and known as a founding figure of the negritude movement in Paris in the 1940s, Senghor astutely maneuvered other left-wing parties, such as Lamine Guèye's socialists, into a series of alliances with his own more nationalist-populist movement. He also managed to secure a lasting alliance with major Sufi leaders, and particularly with Falilou Mbacké, caliph general of the Mouride order. As a result of these multiple alliances, in a 1958 referendum Senegalese voters rejected the possibility of immediate and outright independence in favor of a larger measure of self-rule within the French political system.

Nonetheless, full independence came two years later. The French government dissolved the AOF, and each of the constituent colonies was steered toward full international sovereignty. Many leading African intellectuals, such as Cheikh Anta Diop, condemned the creation of a multiplicity of small, impoverished countries and advocated African unity and a pan-African state.

For a short while, Senegal and Mali (former French Sudan) adhered to this ideal by setting up the Federation of Mali. An agreement to this effect was signed in Paris on April 4, 1960, and the independence of this federation was recognized on June 20. However, Senghor and Malian leader Modibo Keita soon had a falling out, and the federation was dissolved two months later. Senegal and Mali went their separate ways.

POLITICAL CULTURE

Since independence, Senegal has had a centralized, republican, secular, and presidential form of government on the French model, and Senegalese political culture is still largely derived from that of France. Despite authoritarian periods when civil liberties were curtailed, Senegal's government constitutes the longest-running democracy in Africa, and certainly one of the most functional. Essential democratic political freedoms such as freedom of association and freedom of the press have long been entrenched in Senegal. The periods of state repression and authoritarian tendencies, rather benign when compared with most other countries in the region, never succeeded in stifling this fundamentally democratic culture. With political liberalization and democratization accelerating in past decades, civil society has flourished. Local associations, neighborhood associations, youth and sports associations, faith-based organizations, national and international NGOs, and newspapers and radio stations constitute a thick web of exchange, interchange, and advocacy, which underpins contemporary political life.

Democratic institutions and practices have deep roots in Senegal. Already in the eighteenth century the notables of Saint Louis were electing mayors to represent their interests. During the French Revolution the French and Métis inhabitants of Saint Louis and Gorée declared themselves citizens of France, and they pushed this claim again in 1848. By the 1880s, the Four Communes were fully functioning French municipalities where citizens (called *originaires:* French, Métis, and those Africans literate in French) exercised the same rights as their compatriots in France. As a result, civil associations and the free press flourished. Elsewhere in Senegal and French Africa the population had the status of "subject" and enjoyed no such rights.

Politics in the Four Communes was inextricably linked to politics in France itself. French expatriates and the Métis were the first to exercise political rights and freedoms, but at the beginning of the twentieth century, African citizens in the Four Communes, the majority of the electorate, took the lead. The first African political association, the Aurore Club, was established in Saint Louis in 1910. In 1914 Blaise Diagne (1872–1934) became the first African to be elected to the National Assembly in Paris. Diagne was born in Gorée and was of mixed Lebu-Guinean ancestry. His parents were house servants to an influential Métis family. He received a Catholic education and began his career as a civil servant in the customs service, working in a number of French colonies in Africa and the West Indies. No sooner was he elected deputy for Senegal in 1914 than war broke out in Europe. Diagne entered Clemenceau's war cabinet and was put in charge of the recruitment of soldiers in the colonies. As a sitting member of the French National Assembly and cabinet member, Diagne held a status higher than that of the government-appointed governor of Senegal and even of the governor general of the AOF, a situation that caused some official resentment during his frequent visits to Senegal. Diagne was successful in ensuring that recruits from the Four Communes were treated equally with other French soldiers and not like African soldiers with "subject" status. He was also instrumental in supporting the rights of Dakar's Lebu inhabitants in the face of eviction and expropriation by the colonial authorities. After the war, Diagne helped organize the first Pan-African Congress, held in Paris in 1919, where he met W.E.B. Du Bois and Marcus Garvey. In 1924 Diagne was elected mayor of Dakar, though he held on to his deputy's seat in Paris.

Blaise Diagne was not the only influential African politician of his day. Galandou Diouf (1875–1941) was a Muslim Wolof citizen of Saint Louis. Like Diagne, he received a Catholic education. He began his career as a schoolteacher but then turned to journalism. He was on the editorial board of the Dakar daily *La Démocracie* before establishing his own newspapers, *Le Sénégal* and *Le Périscope*. In 1909 he was elected to represent Rufisque on the General Council in Saint Louis, the first African to sit on that colonial body. After Diagne's death in 1934, Galandou Diouf took his seat in the National Assembly. He died in France during the German occupation.

The fall of the Third Republic and the occupation of France by Germany in 1940 brought democratic institutions in Senegal to a standstill. The Vichy regime abolished all its elected councils. When political life resumed after World War II, it was dominated by two men: Lamine Guèye and Léopold Sédar Senghor. Lamine Guèye (1891–1968) was a Muslim citizen of Saint Louis. He studied law in France and became the first African to practice there. He returned to Senegal in 1922 and was elected mayor of Dakar. He ran against Blaise Diagne in the legislative elections of 1928 and against Galandou Diouf in 1934 but failed to defeat either. In 1935 Lamine Guèye set about creating French Africa's first full-fledged political party, the Parti Socialiste Sénégalais (PSS). Following World War II, Guèye joined the Socialist government of Léon Blum in France, where he secured an alliance with the French socialist party, the SFIO. He then handily won the legislative elections of 1946, sitting as deputy for Senegal (the Four Communes) in Paris, where he helped draft legislation that extended citizenship and universal suffrage to all former subjects of the empire.

The extension of the electorate radically changed the dynamics of politics in Senegal, and it heralded the rise of Léopold Sédar Senghor (1906–2001). Unlike his older politician forbearers, Senghor was not born a French citizen. Senghor was Sereer, born in Joal on the Petite Côte. His family was Catholic, and he received a Catholic education in Dakar before departing for France in 1928. He completed a doctorate in French grammar and then began a career in Academia, the first African to do so. During this period he teamed up with Aimé Césaire and Léon Damas, two authors from the French West Indies, in a literary and intellectual movement called negritude. When World War II broke out, Senghor enlisted in the army. He spent two years in German prisoner-of-war camps. After the war, still teaching in France, he was recruited by Lamine Guèye to join the African contingent within France's socialist government. In the newly expanded electoral system, Senghor represented the district of Senegal-Mauritania (which did not include the Four Communes). In 1948, following disagreements over the French government's handling of the AOF railway strike and its bloody repression of the insurrection in Madagascar, Senghor broke with Lamine Guèye and, along with Mamadou Dia (b. 1910), established a new party, the Bloc Démocratique Sénégalais (BDS), and a newspaper, *La Condition Humaine.* In the 1951 elections Lamine Guèye was defeated by Léopold Senghor, who thereafter was a cabinet minister in several of the Fourth Republic's short-lived governments.

The decade of the 1950s was a crucial one. Decolonization was in progress, and there was heated debate on what new political form France's colonies should take. Senghor argued for a federal system encompassing France and all its former colonies. In his view, African nations would do better by maintaining close ties with France. The *loi cadre* of 1956, however, atomized the political structure of this "French Union." Each colony was to exercise limited self-rule, but no democratic institutions were provided for at the federal level. Moreover, in 1958 the AOF as an administrative structure was dissolved. Faced with the new situation, Léopold Senghor and Lamine Guèye agreed to put aside their differences. Their respective parties merged to form the Union Progressiste Sénégalaise (UPS). This political duo successfully negotiated Senegal's accession to independence and the crisis with Mali that soon followed.

Following independence, Senghor, Guèye, and Dia dominated the government. Léopold Senghor, newly elected as president of the republic, concentrated on Senegal's foreign relations and helped establish the Organization of African Unity, among other things. Lamine Guèye, the lawyer, presided over

Senegal's parliament, the National Assembly, and established the legal and constitutional basis of the emerging state. Mamadou Dia, a founding member of the UPS along with Senghor and Guèye, became prime minister. Dia was far more Marxist in his approach than either of his two colleagues. As prime minister, he introduced a radical program of reforms, consisting of rural modernization, economic and social development, and the promotion of grassroots democracy. These policies threatened the interests of the rural-based Sufi orders and proved too radical for Senghor as well. In December 1962 Mamadou Dia was arrested and charged with fomenting a coup. He spent the next 12 years in prison.

Following this political crisis, a second constitution for the republic was drafted and approved by popular referendum in 1963. Loosely modeled on that of de Gaulle's Fifth Republic in France, the new constitution greatly reinforced the powers of the president, and the post of prime minister was abolished. Moreover, while Senegal officially retained the multiparty system, in order to be legal, parties had to gain the state's recognition. Such recognition was not accorded to new parties, and existing parties such as Cheikh Anta Diop's Bloc des Masses Sénégalaises (BMS) and Majhmout Diop's Parti Africain de l'Indépendence (PAI) were banned. Diop's second attempt at creating a political party, the Front National du Sénégal (FNS), met with the same fate. By 1965 there was only one legally recognized political party in Senegal, Senghor's UPS.

Under Senghor's presidency, Senegal had an ambitious cultural policy. Senghor called himself the poet-president. He established negritude and African socialism as guiding state ideologies. In his view, the postcolonial world was to see the emergence of a "Civilization of the Universal," a Métis world-culture that combined the best of Western and African traditions. Consequently, there was great state patronage of the arts: festivals were held, museums were built, and government-financed studios and workshops were established. Yet French remained the only official language, and the only language used in public schools, and state media and government became increasingly elitist and undemocratic.

The unitary, centralized nature of the Republic of Senegal was reinforced by some major legislation. All agricultural property not officially registered with the state was nationalized, putting an effective end to traditional and customary land tenure systems, duties, and privileges. Furthermore, nearly all the traditional aristocratic titles and prerogatives, precolonial in origin but subverted by French colonial rule, were abolished.

In the late 1960s Senegal's colonial-era economic base, the production of peanuts for export, was undermined. First there was a series of severe droughts that affected the entire Sahelo-Sudanic zone, and peanut production declined.

Then the world market price for peanut oil fell, further reducing the state's principal source of revenue. The first sign of social unrest took the form of a general strike in 1968 involving students and unionized workers. The strike was put down militarily, but similar strikes occurred sporadically in subsequent years. Rural areas were also reeling under the economic strain. Farmers found themselves increasingly indebted to the government's peanut marketing board to the point where they could no longer meet their obligations. In 1971 the government was obliged to write off the peasant debt and proceed with agrarian reforms.

Given the deepening economic and social crisis, Senghor began to liberalize the political system. The post of prime minister was resurrected in 1970. In 1974 an opposition party, the Parti Démocratique Sénégalais (PDS), was officially recognized. Led by lawyer Abdoulaye Wade, the PDS had a resolutely liberal platform in opposition to the ruling UPS's officially socialist one. Thereafter, Wade contested every presidential election until his ultimate victory at the polls in 2000. A constitutional amendment in 1976 reestablished the multiparty system, though the state retained the right to withhold recognition of parties. Senghor consolidated the liberalization trend in December 1980 by becoming the first African president to voluntarily resign from office, handing power over to his prime minister, Abdou Diouf. His public life continued, however, as in 1983 the retired poet-president became the first African to be elected to the Académie française, the most prestigious cultural institution in France.

Senghor's hand-picked successor as president was Abdou Diouf, who had been prime minister since 1970. Abdou Diouf's presidency (1981–2000) was marked by continued economic decline, tension with neighboring countries, an armed conflict with Casamance separatists, and the growing role of Islam in public life and discourse. Diouf was a career civil servant, a technocrat upon whom fell the responsibility of implementing the structural adjustment policies dictated to Senegal by international financial institutions. These highly unpopular policies involved the liberalization of the domestic market and the privatization of state-owned enterprises. The cost of living increased sharply as government subsidies for staples such as rice, oil, and sugar ended. In January 1994 the common francophone African currency, the CFA franc, was devalued by half. This further eroded the standard of living of most Senegalese, and by the end of the decade it was estimated that remittances, formal and informal, from Senegalese migrants working abroad had overtaken exports as the country's main source of foreign revenue.

Internationally, Senegal experienced a series of crises under President Diouf. Only months after assuming office, Diouf sent the Senegalese army into neighboring Gambia to thwart a coup attempt against President Jawara.

A Confederation of Senegambia was then set up to foster closer political ties between the two countries, but no permanent institutions were ever created and it was discreetly dissolved in 1989. That same year, relations with neighboring Mauritania descended into violence. A dispute over transborder grazing rights and water use escalated, leading to 400 deaths and tens of thousands of minority nationals in each country being repatriated as refugees. Meanwhile, the ethnically based secessionist conflict in the Lower Casamance, which had erupted in December 1982, continued unabated.

Despite these grave problems, President Diouf strove to enhance Senegal's international profile. Dakar hosted important international summits such as the Francophonie in 1989 and the Organization of the Islamic Conference in 1991. Senegal joined the UN-backed international coalition against Iraq in the 1991 Gulf War, and Abdou Diouf served a term as chairman of the Organization of African Unity in 1992–1993.

Senegalese democracy struggled under Diouf. Officially, political pluralism and the multiparty system were said to be fully functioning. Yet, presidential and legislative elections were tense affairs. Though Abdou Diouf and the Parti socialiste (or PS, the rebaptized UPS) continued to win elections, the legitimacy of these elections was regularly contested. Opposition leaders often found themselves in prison, and political organizations could easily be banned. The February 1988 presidential elections were particularly bitter. For a moment, Abdou Diouf appeared to be restoring Senghor's strategic alliance with the Mouride order when Caliph General Abdoul Ahad Mbacké publicly called on Mourides to vote for the president and his Socialist Party. This was, however, the last time a Senegalese religious authority took such a political stand. Following the announcement of results on election night, Dakar's youth took to the streets in protest. Diouf declared a state of emergency in the capital, and Abdoulaye Wade, leader of the opposition PDS, was arrested.

Senegal's democratic credentials, however, were confirmed during the 2000 presidential elections when Abdou Diouf was resoundingly defeated by Abdoulaye Wade in the second round. This was the first instance of an election producing a change of government (*alternance* in French) in sub-Saharan Africa since independence. After a dignified transition of power, Diouf was elected secretary general of the Francophonie, where he is now serving his second four-year term. A new Senegalese constitution, which aims at decentralizing power toward regions and municipalities and which reduces the mandate of the president to two five-year terms, was approved by referendum in January 2001. In parliamentary elections in April of that year, Wade's PDS-led coalition took a majority of seats, and the PS found itself in opposition for the first time since independence.

Following on the painful structural adjustment policies of the Diouf era, Wade has pursued economic liberalization characterized by a free-market, open-door approach and the creation of an investor-friendly climate. Private investments have been sought in the transportation and communications sectors, while the country's fledgling tourism industry has also been promoted for foreign direct investment. Abdoulaye Wade calls his political-economic policies the "emergence" of Senegal. One of his major achievements has been in Casamance, where, after more than two decades, the conflict seems to have been resolved. In December 2004 most parties involved signed a peace and reconstruction agreement; only one small rebel faction continues to fight the Senegalese army.

Abdoulaye Wade won a second term in office in the first round of the 2007 presidential elections, but the legislative elections later that year were boycotted by the main opposition parties. Moreover, the great expectations for liberal economic growth have yet to be realized. Lower-and middle-income Senegalese families continue to experience declining purchasing power and daily hardships, and young people remain generally disillusioned with politics.

2

Religion

Senegal is a Muslim country, and though it is a secular state, Islamic institutions and practices dominate the public sphere and public space. The great majority of Senegalese—94 percent, according to official government sources—are Sunni Muslims who follow the Maliki school of Islamic law. Notwithstanding this statistic, there is a great deal of religious diversity within the country. First of all, the Muslim community is subdivided into a number of Sufi orders, or brotherhoods, that have quite distinct traditions and histories. Second, there is a sizable Christian community in Senegal consisting of about half a million people, or 5 percent of the national population. It is composed mainly of Catholics. The small percentage of Christians, however, does not accurately reflect the influence and position of this religion in the public sphere. The Christian community is overwhelmingly concentrated in Senegal's largest and oldest cities—Dakar, Saint Louis, and Thiès—or it is embedded within Diola and Sereer ethnicity. Official government sources also claim that about 1 percent of Senegalese follow "traditional" religion—that is, they are neither Muslim nor Christian and they practice locally based rites related to the spirit world. Such traditional religious practices have virtually no visibility in the public sphere. Traditional religion is practiced in rather isolated rural areas in the south, among the Bassari and the Balant. On the other hand, certain deeply embedded popular beliefs about the spirit world, also considered to be traditional, are shared across religious divides. Acceptance of religious diversity and recognition of the underlying commonality of all religious beliefs form the basis of interfaith relations in Senegal, which has greatly contributed to maintaining social peace in the country over the last 100 years.

TRADITIONAL AFRICAN RELIGION

Traditional African religion is practiced today by about 100,000 people, according to government sources. These practices can be characterized in a variety of ways. In the past, the term "animism" was often applied. Animism refers to the belief that spirits inhabit, or animate, objects. Typically, these objects are features of the landscape such as trees, groves, rocks, ponds, riverbanks, and islands. These location-specific spirits, called *tuur* in Wolof and *pangool* in Sereer, are influential in daily life, whether it be agriculture and animal husbandry, family life, or individual health. To assuage these potentially malefic spirits, they are placated with sacrificial offerings, usually of meat or animal blood.

In some cases, full-fledged shrines are maintained at the sites inhabited by such spirits. Shrine attendants, either men or women of a specific family, monitor the offerings and enact secret rites passed down from earlier generations. A village quarter, an entire village, or a group of villages may recognize a given spirit as its patron. The oral traditions of the Wolof and Sereer tell us that, historically, a class of priests existed to minister to the spirits. These priests were present at court and held political positions, even if the king happened to be Muslim. In such cases, traditional religion was very much part of the public sphere. In the precolonial era, certain shrines, often marked by large trees, were the object of public rituals and assemblies attended by court officials, regional representatives, and military officers.

Shrines might also contain a fetish, hence the use of the terms "fetishism" and "fetishist" to designate traditional religion. A fetish is a small sculptural figure usually made of wood and adorned with cowries, feathers, beads, and paint. It is a representation of, or conduit to, the spirit and is kept concealed in the shrine. Only the priest may see or minister to the fetish, or alter its adornments. Very few fetish shrines exist in Senegal today, and it may never have been a widespread religious practice.

Far more common in Senegal are sacred groves. These forests are located at the edge of a village or between several villages, and they are home to their patron spirit. Sacred groves are used mostly for initiation rites, when pubescent or adolescent boys become men. Initiation is a long process lasting weeks or even months and involving circumcision and the learning of secret knowledge about life forces. During initiation, the boys are secluded in the grove and supervised by one or two elders. Initiation is always collective. It occurs once in a generation when a whole cohort of boys is initiated together, creating a strong bond that will last the rest of their lives. Before colonial conquest ended local warfare, cohorts of adult warriors returned to the sacred grove before battle to prepare spiritually and mentally for the coming ordeal.

Traditional religion has also been called ancestral and totemic. The ancestral nature of this religion lies in the fact that it is acquired from one's parents and not from a holy book such as the Koran or the Bible, and that the spirits of one's departed ancestors are still relevant to daily life. However, ancestor worship, the creation of shrines and offerings to the ancestors, has never been a common practice in Senegal. The totemic nature of traditional religion lies in the belief that lineages are protected by an animal patron spirit. It is commonly believed, for example, that the Ndiaye (one of the most common and aristocratic Senegalese family names) belong to the lion. While this belief may have been more widespread in the past, at no time did it involve the actual worship of animals.

It is certain that in the distant past, before the introduction of Islam and Christianity, all of Senegal's ethnic groups practiced some form of traditional religion. However, it is practiced today mostly among the historically acephalous groups, such as the Balant and the Bassari, and to a much lesser extent among the Diola and the Sereer. Also, because it is so place specific—the beliefs and practices being linked to specific places—traditional religion does not migrate well. When individuals or families who practice it move to another region or to a city in search of work, they cannot maintain most of the rites and rituals and they tend to adopt Muslim or Christian practices instead.

ISLAM AND SUFI ORDERS

Today, Islam is the religion of the great majority of Senegalese. Its presence in the country is also quite ancient: Islam was practiced in the kingdom of Takrur by the eleventh century, when its king, War Jaabi, adopted the faith. Throughout most of Senegal's history, however, Islam has been the religion of a minority. The first to convert appeared to have been aristocrats, princes, and people of noble birth. Islam then adopted a dual character. On the one hand, it constituted an important faction at court, evolving in the antechambers of power. On the other hand, Islam thrived in autonomous, self-governing villages set up by teachers in relative isolation from political currents. Islam may have become the religion of the majority of the population of Takrur by the fifteenth century, but in most states farther south it remained the religion of a minority until well into the nineteenth century. Muslims and practitioners of traditional religion thus shared the public political and social sphere, and not always peacefully, for many centuries. Islam only became the religion of the majority of the population at about the time Senegal was being colonized by the French.

The form of Islam that dominated religious practice in the mid to late nineteenth century was Sufism. The term "Sufism" refers to the esoteric, mystical dimensions of Islam. Certain pious Muslims have always sought a deeper understanding of God than that which can be obtained through practicing the five pillars of the faith: the *shahâdah* (witnessing God's oneness and the prophetic stature of Muhammad), *salâh* (praying five times a day), *zakâh* (giving alms), *sawm* (fasting during the month of Ramadan), and *hajj* (making a pilgrimage to Mecca for those who are able). A number of additional religious practices, such as *dhikr* (remembering God by reciting his names), *samâ'* (reciting poems, singing praise songs), and *hadrah* (moving the body), are available to those wanting to grow closer to God. These activities are often conducted in groups (groups of men and groups of women separately, more rarely mixed groups). These Sufi practices are promoted and coordinated by distinct institutions, called *tarîqahs,* literally "ways" but better translated as Sufi brotherhoods, or "orders."

Sufi practices and Sufi orders were present among the literate elite of Senegal's Muslim population before the nineteenth century. However, it is during the late nineteenth century, at the time of colonial conquest, that some members of this elite turned the Sufi orders into mass movements. Today, virtually all Muslims in Senegal claim an affiliation to one Sufi order or another. Senegal's Sufi orders are thus among the principal institutions of its civil society. They are central to social relations, cultural expression, and economics and politics, and they have been extensively studied by social scientists.

Though Senegal's various Sufi orders are not all exactly alike, they share many common characteristics. Typically, the order is headed by a caliph (*khalîfah* in Arabic) who is a direct male descendant of the order's founder and who has inherited his forefather's *barakah* (divine grace). Below the caliph are various sheikhs or *muqàddams,* literally "elders," responsible for a specific constituency within the order. Since the colonial period, the French term "marabout" has designated these Muslim clerics, but this term can have derogatory connotations (equivalent to "charlatan"). These sheikhs have usually also inherited their positions from their fathers. In some rare cases, women can hold the position of sheikh. Finally, the rank-and-file members of the orders, male and female, are referred to as *taalibes* or *murits;* they are students or seekers of the Sufi way. A *taalibe* always has a sheikh, a spiritual elder who gives guidance. The relationship, however, is far more complex. A *taalibe* may ask his or her sheikh for help in times of need (family crisis, financial crises, etc.), while a sheikh may request special service from a *taalibe* or send the *taalibe* on a mission. The relationship is also monetary. A *taalibe* is expected to donate money or gifts in kind (called *addiya*) to his or her sheikh, who, in return, is expected to be generous to *taalibes* in need. Children are socialized into a Sufi order early on, being assigned a sheikh from among those known to the parents and then attending that sheikh's Koranic school. While one's Sufi affiliation is thus inherited from one's parents, it is not unheard of for a *taalibe* to choose a new sheikh or join a different Sufi order altogether. Senegal has four Sufi orders: the Qadiriyya, the Tijaniyya, the Mourides, and the Layène.

The Qadiriyya order, pronounced "Khadr" in Wolof, is the oldest order in Senegal. It gets its name from 'Abd al-Qâdr al-Jîlânî (1077–1166), a celebrated mystic whose tomb in Baghdad is still the order's principal shrine. The Qadiriyya was first introduced in Senegal by Mauritanian teachers, and Mauritania is still important to this order's current operations. The main Qadiri group in Senegal was established by Sheikh Bou Kounta (1844–1914) in the town of Ndiassane. Two Mauritanian branches of this order are also very active in Senegal: the Fadhiliya branch of Sheikh Sa'ad Bûh b. Muhammad al-Fâdhil (1850–1917) in Nimjat and the Sidiyya branch of Sheikh Sidiyya al-Kabîr (1780–1868) in Boutilimit. It is estimated that about 10 percent of Senegal's Muslims (about 900,000 people) are members of the Qadiriyya.

The Tijaniyya order, founded by Sîdî Ahmad al-Tijânî (1737–1815) in Fez, Morocco, became a major political and social force in Senegambia in the mid-nineteenth century. All the leaders of the jihads of that time—Al-Hajj Umar Tall (1797–1864), Maba Diakhou (1809–1867), and Cheikhou Ahmadou Mahdiyou Baa (1820–1875)—were sheikhs of the Tijaniyya. Today, about 50 percent of Senegalese Muslims (about 5 million people) claim affiliation to some branch of the Tijaniyya. Like the Qadiriyya, the Tijaniyya is subdivided into a number of distinct branches that function independently of one another. The Tivaouane, or Malikiyya, branch was established by Al-Hajj Malick Sy (1855–1922). It has a national, and especially an urban, following. The Kaolack, or Niassène, branch of the Tijaniyya was established by Al-Hajj Abdoulaye Niass (1844–1922), but it was his son, Al-Hajj Ibrahima Niass (1900–1975), who turned it into an international organization. This branch calls itself the Jama'at al-Faydah and has members across West Africa as well as in the United States, among African Americans especially. Other branches of the Tijaniyya include the Mahdiyya of Tiénaba, established by Amary Ndack Seck (1830–1899), and the Madina Gounass Tijaniyya, established by Al-Hajj Tierno Mamadou Seydou Baa (1898–1980).

By far the most famous and most studied Sufi order in Senegal is that of the Mourides, sometimes called the Muridiyya. It was established by Sheikh

Ahmadou Bamba Mbacké (1853–1927), who is buried in Touba, the holy city of the Mourides. It is estimated that there are about 3 million Mourides. They are mostly in Senegal, but some now live elsewhere, in West Africa, in Western Europe, and in North America. In contrast to the Qadiriyya and Tijaniyya orders, the Mourides are a homegrown Sufi order, not having diffused from elsewhere in the Arab-Muslim world. Also in contrast to the other two, the Mourides are not subdivided into independent branches. The order has a strong centralized and hierarchic structure and recognizes only one caliph general, a grandson of Sheikh Ahmadou Bamba who resides in Touba.

Also homegrown is the tiny Layène order, whose membership is estimated at between 20,000 and 30,000. This order was established by Seydina Mouhammadou Limamou Laye (1844–1909) in Yoff, now a suburb of Dakar, and its membership is almost entirely limited to the Lebu of the Cape Vert Peninsula.

Though they are roughly contemporaneous with one another, each of Senegal's Sufi orders has a distinct history and social basis. The Tijaniyya, for example, attracted a large urban and middle-class following during the colonial period and was well represented in the country's civil service following independence. It also predominates among the Halpulaaren and in the Futa Toro. The Mourides, on the other hand, began as a rural and peasant movement in the Wolof heartland of Baol and Kayor, where it also assimilated members of the old landed aristocracy. In recent decades it has become increasingly urban, with many merchants and entrepreneurs among its members. The Qadiriyya found a niche among Senegal's ethnic minority groups: Mauritanians living in Senegal, migrant Bambara railway workers from Mali, Mandika of the central Casamance, and so forth.

Each Sufi order maintains one or more shrines, usually related to the tomb of the founder. Some of these, such as Touba and Madina Gounass, are full-fledged cities—in fact, these two Sufi cities have autonomous status within Senegal. In other cases the shrines constitute distinct neighborhoods within large cities, as in Tivaouane and Kaolack, or they are located in small towns and villages. Senegal is dotted with such Sufi shrines, and all of them date from the late nineteenth and early twentieth centuries. They are considered holy places. Proper Islamic decorum prevails, and neither alcohol nor tobacco consumption is permitted. The shrines are also the locus of numerous religious festivals and commemorations, called *siyaares, gàmmus,* and *màggals.* Each of these mass events is held annually, usually according to the Islamic calendar, and they constitute major religious, social, and economic occasions. Senegal's Sufi shrine centers, great and small, are also important educational centers. Primary education begins in the *daara,* or Koranic school. Afterward, students can attend any number of institutes of higher Islamic instruction located in places like Koki, Pire Gourey, Louga, Fass Touré, Touba, and Kaolack.

Touba is, undoubtedly, Senegal's most impressive Sufi city. With about half a million inhabitants, it is the country's second largest city. It is also an autonomous city. Ever since it was founded in 1887 by Sheikh Ahmadou Bamba Mbacké in a moment of mystic illumination, the Mouride sheikhs have tightly controlled its construction and development and have successfully restricted the ability of government agencies to intervene within its precincts. It is the Mouride order that is responsible for the laying of streets, the allotment of residential subdivisions, water distribution, schools, hospitals, markets, and so forth. Religion is Touba's raison d'être and is at the heart of all its activities. The city's skyline is dominated by the Great Mosque, which rises at its center. There are countless Koranic schools and several institutes of higher Islamic education; Touba is renowned for its quality of Arabic instruction. It is also famous for its pilgrimages, the main one being the Grand Màggal, which attracts well over a million people each year.

Senegal's Sufi orders are especially important to its contemporary popular culture. The founders of the orders are considered heroes; their exploits are the subject of songs, and their portraits are reproduced in every conceivable medium. The Sufi orders themselves are ubiquitous in society. Sheikhs are influential well beyond the confines of the shrine towns. For their part, the rank-and-file members of the orders are organized in a multitude of associations called *dahiras*. *Dahiras* can be organized by the followers of a specific sheikh or by members of a particular order in a given neighborhood or business. Women manage their own *dahiras*. The primary activity of most *dahiras* consists of evenings of Sufi recitation, called *njàng*. *Dahiras* can also involve themselves in charitable work, for example, helping to pay medical or funeral expenses of members.

CHRISTIANITY AND THE CATHOLIC CHURCH

Christianity has been present in Senegal since the fifteenth century, when Portuguese traders introduced Catholicism. The first Christian communities were those of the Lançados, descendants of Portuguese traders and African women, established in the ports of the Petite Côte: Rufisque, Portudal, and Joal. The Catholic Church, however, was unable to provide these communities with certified priests; thus, they were ministered to only occasionally, by traveling priests from the Cape Verde Islands. The French, who had more secure positions in Gorée and Saint Louis, were able to establish permanent Catholic institutions. As with the Lançados, Catholicism was adopted by the

Franco-African Métis communities. Saint Louis, especially, acquired several important Catholic institutions, including a congregation of the Sisters of Saint Joseph of Cluny and a cathedral that was built in 1828. By the 1840s Senegalese men were being ordained as priests. With the onset of official French colonization in the 1880s, French Catholic missionary institutions, based in the Four Communes, became active in the interior. To maintain social peace in the conquered hinterland, colonial authorities prohibited Christian missionary work in Muslim areas. The missionaries thus concentrated their efforts among the Sereer and in the lower Casamance, among the Diola. The mission schools, which operated entirely in French, served as conduits to the civil service during colonial rule. By independence, Catholics held important political and administrative positions. Leopold Sédar Senghor, the first president of Senegal, was a Sereer Catholic.

The distribution of Senegal's Catholic community, estimated at about half a million people, reflects this history. It is predominantly an urban community, concentrated in Dakar, Saint Louis, Thiès, and Ziguinchor, where the main cathedrals are located. There are also cathedrals in Kaolack, Kolda, and Tambacounda. Dakar is exceptionally well endowed with private Catholic schools and colleges, though many of the students are Muslim. Dakar's small but influential Maronite Lebanese community is a strong backer of Catholic institutions. The Congrégation du Saint Esprit, established at Ngazobil on the Petite Côte in 1850, is an important educational institution. There is a Catholic shrine in Popenguine, also on the Petite Côte, where an annual pilgrimage is held. Cardinal Hyacinthe Thiandoum (1921–2004), Senegal's most famous Catholic cleric, was from Popenguine.

Relations between Senegalese Muslims and Christians have always been cordial and respectful. Nineteenth-century jihads mostly pitted Muslims against other Muslims, and occasionally against traditionalists, but not against Christians. Leopold Sédar Senghor's remarkable political success was his ability to secure the backing of all of Senegal's Sufi caliphs against his Muslim political rivals. More than one Muslim cleric today sends his children to a private Catholic school in order to get a solid Jesuitical education. Muslims see the Catholic Church in Senegal as equivalent to a Sufi order, with its own clerical hierarchy, schools, and pilgrimage centers. Intermarriage between Muslims and Christians, while not exactly common, is not entirely unheard of either. There are interesting borrowings as well. The traditional "naming" ceremony of a Muslim child, which takes place on the seventh or eighth day after birth, is commonly called a baptism. The Layène Sufi order holds Jesus (or "Issa"), recognized as an important messenger of God by Muslims in any case, in particularly high regard and holds a commemorative celebration each Christmas. Senegal's official motto, adopted at independence, states,

"One people, one aim, one faith"; the various religions present in Senegal are thus seen as expressions of a single faith. The knowledge that Muslims, Christians, and traditionalists ultimately worship the same God, though in different ways, forms the basis of interfaith relations.

POPULAR BELIEFS

Many Senegalese hold a number of beliefs related to the spirit world that are quite distinct from the religious practices and observances transmitted through organized religions. These beliefs are best described as popular. They are widely held and appear to be timeless, having no perceivable origin or source. Moreover, they are shared across the religious divides, by Muslims, Christians, and traditionalists alike.

Among the most widespread of popular beliefs is that a variety of non-human spirits inhabit the world and must be dealt with. Some of these spirits, the *tuur,* inhabit certain places and have authority over them. This belief is obviously important to practitioners of traditional African religion, but it also characterizes many places inhabited entirely by Muslims or Christians. In Popenguine, a Catholic pilgrimage site with a large Muslim population, the *tuur* is named Coumb Cupaam, while in Yoff, a Sufi shrine town in the suburbs of Dakar, the *tuur* is named Mame Ndiaré and takes the form of a bird. *Tuurs* are patron spirits. They are known to the inhabitants, who respect them and fear them in equal measure. In Rufisque, a road accident or a drowning will result if the *tuur* Mame Coumba Lambaye is not placated. One keeps one's distance from a *tuur* if at all possible and avoids the places where they reside. Only members of specific lineages approach these haunts, which are generally left isolated and undeveloped. In Kaolack, the *tuur* takes the form of a *bar,* a large amphibious monitor lizard, called Mboose. Only the female descendants of the two Sereer princesses from Baol, who founded Kaolack, can officiate on the riverbank where Mboose lives. Yet this ceremony is preceded by a very popular public procession in the city center involving music and dance. Occasionally, a *tuur* can have a debonair reputation, such as Dakar's Ndek Dawur, who will suddenly appear from nowhere to help someone in distress. In Saint Louis the *tuur* has the form of a woman, sometimes old, sometimes young, called Mame Coumba Bang. Those who catch a glimpse of her, always from a distance, consider themselves blessed.

Another type of spirit is the *rab,* or *pangool* in Sereer. A *rab* is a "free" spirit (equivalent to the Islamic concept of jinn), not fixed to a single place or lineage, that can attach itself to an individual or to some random place for any number of reasons and cause much trauma. An individual "possessed" in this way, or one who has inadvertently disturbed a *rab,* requires the specialized skills of a traditional healer or a Sufi sheikh in order to exorcise it. In effect, many Senegalese prefer to use the services of traditional healers and sheikhs when dealing with physical or mental health issues rather than submit to Western medicine or doctors and psychiatrists trained in the Western tradition.

Many popular beliefs and practices relate to mental and physical health. Individuals seek to protect themselves from illness, accidents, and the evil intentions of others through charms and talismans, called *téere* in Wolof (equivalent to terms such as "juju," "mojo," and "gris-gris"). These charms come in a variety of forms, and many are worn on the body. Bound in leather they can belt the waist or ring the neck or a bicep. Encased in silver they are worn as rings and bracelets. They can also be buried in the earth or hung from a tree, depending on the provenance of the perceived threat. *Téere* are manufactured either by traditional healers or by Muslim sheikhs (marabouts), in which case they will contain Koranic phrases or esoteric configurations of Arabic letters and numbers, referred to as *xaatims* or "magic squares." Historically, the warrior caste (the *ceddo*) was a great consumer of such charms, mainly produced by Muslim clerics, as they required great amounts of protection in battle. Today, many athletes in all sports employ talismans, as do politicians (or so it is rumored). Children are especially vulnerable to unprovoked evil and are therefore protected by *téere* almost from the moment of birth.

While religiously educated and orthodox-minded Muslim and Christian clerics, as well as Senegal's secular educated elite, may disapprove of these popular beliefs and practices, they are widely held by ordinary people of all faiths who see no contradiction in holding to them while practicing a formal religion like Islam or Christianity.

3

Literature, Academics, and Media

SENEGAL'S LITERARY AND cinematographic tradition is rooted in three main sources: the country's rich orature, Islamic scholarship, and the long French colonial experience. The oral traditions of Senegal's various ethnic groups and historic kingdoms provide many of the narrative modes for contemporary novels, plays, and films. Arabic was Senegal's first literary language, and it is still used for religious poetry. The long cohabitation with the French language and with French civilization as it was promoted in the colony has deeply imprinted artistic expression and continues to do so to this day, especially in published works and the print media.

ORATURE AND THE GRIOTS

As elsewhere in West Africa, Senegal's oral traditions were developed and transmitted by a specific professional caste, that of the griots. "Griot" is a French term that, like "marabout," is now ubiquitous in English-language literature. The Wolof term is *géwél*. Griots have been called praise singers, and the term "griotism" today can have negative connotations, designating commentators, journalists, or artists who laud those in power. Griots have also been called bards, by analogy to the oral and musical traditions of Celtic Europe and archaic Greece. Senegal's modern-day griots call themselves traditional communicators and are represented by a national professional association.

Griots were the historians and chroniclers of the precolonial era. They composed histories and recited them to the accompaniment of music. The stories were in prose or in verse and recounted epic exploits of battle, illustrious genealogies, or foundation myths. Such orature was a sociological and political necessity; every village, every aristocratic family, every great warrior had its griot. Some griots were attached to specific lineages or to the royal courts. Griots performed publicly, in front of an audience, and their stories were tailored to the needs of a particular audience and occasion. Griots were protective of their specialized knowledge and transmitted it secretly, within the family, from one generation to the next. Both men and women were griots.

Senegal's precolonial griot tradition lives on in a variety of contemporary cultural expressions, including in Islamic practice. Whereas griots used to sing of brave warriors and heroic kings, today they sing the praises of Senegal's famous Sufis, and of Sheikh Ahmadou Bamba Mbacké in particular. They also sing the praises of living Sufi sheikhs, the caliphs of the orders, and other charismatic religious leaders. Successful businesspeople, athletes, and politicians on the make may also patronize griots, though the attention is not always welcome. One must be very generous toward a griot who sings one's praises; gifts of expensive cars and gold jewelry are preferred. A patron who fails to reward a griot is jinxed—or worse, the griot might publicly ridicule the miserly patron through scathing verse, greatly damaging the patron's reputation.

All in all, the griot tradition has provided much of what we know about precolonial history and politics, at the level of whole states and kingdoms as well as at the level of specific lineages and individual villages. In the early twentieth century, several griots bequeathed written accounts of their historical narratives, either in French, such as Yoro Dyao's *Chronicles of Kayor* and Alioune Sarr's *History of Sine-Saloum,* or in Wolof, such as Assane Marokhaya Samb's *Essai on the History of Kayor.* Such texts still serve as sources for the writing of history by today's historians. Nowadays, celebrated griots are invited to discuss Senegal's history on radio and TV. Moreover, the entertainment dimension of the griot tradition is still a powerful force in show business and pop culture. Some of Senegal's most successful contemporary female singers, such as Maada Thiam, Fatou Guewel, and Kiné Lam, come from griot families.

Not all precolonial orature was created by griots. The sage Kocc Barma (1584–1654) was of noble birth and a member of Kayor's ruling Fall lineage. He was a councillor to King Madior Fatim Goleň (reigned 1647–1664) and is remembered for four Wolof aphorisms: (1) love women but never trust them, (2) a king has no kin, (3) an adopted son is not a true son, and (4) elders are needed in the village. These aphorisms related directly to court politics and power relations within the ruling dynasty. The circumstances under which Kocc Barma formulated and then expressed them are taught to schoolchildren. He is regarded as a folk hero and is featured in many songs, plays, and TV shows. A cenotaph-mausoleum in his honor was recently built in Njongué, Kocc Barma's home village.

LITERATURE IN ARABIC AND WOLOFAL

Literacy in Arabic must have appeared in Senegal at the same time as Islam itself, and it became more and more common as Islam spread geographically, sociologically, and demographically. Books in Arabic, related to the religious sciences—the *sunna* (traditions of the prophet Muhammad), *fiqh* (jurisprudence), grammar and philology, astronomy, and so forth—imported from north of the Sahara were circulating throughout Senegal by the seventeenth century and were used for pedagogical purposes. The oldest surviving works in Arabic by a Senegalese author were written by a famous nineteenth-century scholar and judge, Kali Madiakhaté Kala (1835–1902), chief justice at the court of King Lat Dior. He wrote religious poetry, in both Arabic and Wolof, as well as political treatises.

The next generation of Senegalese authors to compose original works in Arabic consisted of Sufi sheikhs. The most prolific Sufi writer was one of Kali Madiakhaté Kala's students, Sheikh Ahmadou Bamba Mbacké, founder of the Mouride order. Ahmadou Bamba wrote dozens of odes (a poetic form called *qasîdah* in Arabic) on a wide range of religious themes. These odes are published in small pocketbook format. Inexpensive to purchase, they are widely known and recited by Mourides during collective evening events, called *njàng*, organized by *dahiras*. Other Senegalese Sufi poets who composed in Arabic include Al-Hajj Malick Sy (1855–1922), founder of the Tivaouane branch of the Tijaniyya; Al-Hajj Ahmadou Momar Niass (1881–1957), who was caliph of the Kaolack Tijaniyya; Al-Hajj Abdoul Aziz Sy (1904–1997), caliph of the Tivaouane Tijaniyya; and Sheikh Hadi Touré (1894–1979) and his sons Abdoul Aziz and Malick of Fass, who are also Tijanis.

Not all of Senegal's Arabic-language literature is poetic, or even religious. Moussa Kamara (1863–1943) wrote a number of important historical essays about his homeland, Futa Toro, and about Sufi institutions and leaders of the nineteenth century. These works include *Zuhûr al-Basâtîn* (written in 1924–1925) and a text in Pulaar, the *Tarih Hayri Labi*. His contemporary, Sheikh Mbacké Bousso (1864–1945), was a major intellectual figure of the Mouride order and wrote numerous political essays in Arabic. Much of the work of these two authors has been translated into French.

One of the spin-off effects of literacy in Arabic has been the development of literature in national languages, Pulaar and Wolof in particular, through use of an adapted form of the Arabic alphabet called the 'ajâmî script. The Wolof version of this alphabet is called Wolofal. It was in use prior to French colonization and continues to be used today in religious contexts, and in Touba in particular, despite the fact that normative Wolof is now written in a derivative Latin alphabet.

Religious poetry accounts for a large proportion of works in Wolofal as classical Islamic themes and Arabic metrics are adapted to the Wolof language. And, once again, many Wolofal authors are Sufi sheikhs. Both Sheikh Hadi Touré and Al-Hajj Abdoul Aziz Sy, mentioned earlier for their Arabic poetry, wrote odes in Wolof, as did Kali Madiakhaté Kala. The most famous Wolofal poet was Sheikh Moussa Ka (1891–1966), a disciple of Ahmadou Bamba. *Barzakh* and *Jazâ' Sakûr* constitute his major works. Other Mouride poets include Mbaye Diakhaté, More Khaïré (1869–1951), Samba Diarra Mbaye (1870–1917), Cheikh Fall Trahir, and Sokhna Maïmouna Mbacké (1926–2000), Ahmadou Bamba's youngest daughter. Contrary to Sheikh Ahmadou Bamba's Arabic-language odes, which circulate in published form, the poems of these "Wolofalkats" (the term used to designate Wolof poets) circulate mostly in audio form, recorded on cassettes. Until recently they were not taken seriously as a literary genre, but they are now appreciated in literary circles and are the subject of academic research.

FRENCH INTELLECTUAL CULTURE

The third source of contemporary Senegalese cultural expression is French. Nineteenth-century France pursued an "assimilationist" policy in its overseas colonies. French civilization was considered universally valid. Thus anyone, including colonial subjects in Africa and the West Indies (the French Antilles), could be educated in it and become French. Furthermore, Senegal's Four Communes were legally part of metropolitan French territory, and their inhabitants enjoyed the same duties and privileges as other French citizens. Consequently, a small elite of French-educated intellectuals (lawyers, doctors, journalists) emerged, first in Saint Louis and Gorée, then in Dakar.

By the inter-war period, Paris itself was home to many Senegalese intellectuals who contributed, along with black West Indians and expatriate African Americans, to a renaissance of African cultural expression. This Parisian renaissance, immortalized by Josephine Baker, was in every way the counterpart to the contemporaneous Harlem Renaissance in the United States. Pan-African congresses, attended by W.E.B. Du Bois, among many other intellectuals, were held in Paris in 1919 and 1921. These events greatly influenced Senegalese artists and intellectuals.

The first Senegalese authors of works in French were Amadou Ndiaye Dugay Cledor (1886–1937), Amadou Mapathe Diagne (1890–1976), and Bakary Diallo (1892–1980). They wrote novels, short stories, and books for children that, to various degrees, expressed support for the colonial system and the benefits of French civilization. A more critical stance was adopted by Massyla Diop (1885–1932) and his brother Birago (1906–1989). Massyla Diop wrote poems and novels, and he edited a Parisian literary journal in the 1920s in which he advocated the rehabilitation of African values and traditions. Birago Diop, a veterinarian by profession, wrote poetry inspired by the tales of Senegalese griots. He was also an active member of the intellectual circle that eventually produced the negritude movement. This circle included his compatriots Ousmane Socé Diop (1911–1961) and Léopold Sédar Senghor as well as Aimé Césaire from Martinique (b. 1913), Léon Damas from French Guyana (1912–1978), and Jacques Rabemananjara of Madagascar (1913–2005). These authors rejected assimilationism in favor of a foundation in African culture. They did not, however, reject French civilization. Rather, they called for an association of French and African culture within a universal Métis civilization. Socé Diop, who like Senghor had both a political and literary career, drew inspiration from Wolof aphorism and proverbs, folk songs, traditional religious practices, and tales of the griots, whereas Senghor drew extensively from his boyhood experience in rural Sine.

One of the foremost Senegalese intellectuals of the Paris Renaissance was Alioune Diop (1910–1980), founder of *Présence africaine*. *Présence africaine* began as a literary journal in 1947 and eventually became a major publishing house for contemporary African literature and scholarship. Alioune Diop steered negritude through the potential pitfalls of a tense political era, that of decolonization and the cold war. In 1956 he presided over the First Congress of Black Writers and Artists, a pan-African event held in Paris and attended by the American authors Richard Write and James Baldwin. Following independence he moved to Dakar and pursued his cultural construction activities across Africa. *Présence africaine,* however, continued to publish out of Paris and remained at the cutting edge of African literary production. Cheikh Anta Diop, the leading Senegalese academic of his generation, published exclusively with *Présence africaine.*

Cheikh Anta Diop (1923–1986) was the first Black African to study Egyptology, after having first studied physics. His groundbreaking doctoral dissertation on the Black African identity of Pharaonic civilization was rejected by the jury of Paris's Sorbonne University in 1951. In response, he had the study published as *Nations nègres et culture* by *Présence africaine,* ensuring a wide distribution. Around the time of independence, he wrote in quick succession *L'unité culturelle de l'Afrique Noire* and *L'Afrique Noire précoloniale,* in which he laid out a blueprint of a politically united, culturally grounded continent. Cheikh Anta Diop's militant support for Africa's political unification after independence—twice he set up political parties (the Bloc des Masses Sénégalaises in 1961 and the Front National du Sénégal in 1964) for this purpose—won him the enmity of President Senghor. Both parties were banned. His scholarly career at the University of Dakar, where he set up a radiocarbon dating laboratory for archeological research, had a far happier outcome. When Cheikh Anta Diop died in 1986, Dakar's university was renamed after him.

CONTEMPORARY LITERATURE

Literary production flourished in Dakar following Senegal's independence. Authors included Malick Fall (1920–1978), Lamine Diakhaté (1928–1987), Cheikh Aliou Ndao (b. 1933), Abdou Anta Ka (b. 1931), and Amadou Traore Diop (b. 1944). These authors passed freely between genres and they built on the methods of negritude by drawing inspiration from various traditional themes from Senegal's precolonial history. They were, however, concerned with the pressing issues of their generation, issues such as rural-urban migration, urban alienation, global ideological confrontations, and the continued struggle of most Senegalese to put food on the table each day.

The works of Senegal's first woman author, Annette Mbaye d'Erneville (b. 1926), also date from this period. Educated in the Catholic institutions of Saint Louis and Rufisque, she went on to study journalism in Paris after World War II, where, like other Senegalese students of her generation, she got caught up in the Paris Renaissance. Upon returning to Senegal in 1957 she helped create *Femmes de soleil* (later rebaptized *Awa*), Senegal's first women's magazine, and then began writing poems and children's stories, a literary activity she pursues today.

Two authors of the independence generation, Cheikh Hamidou Kane and Ousmane Sembène, have received much international acclaim. Cheikh Hamidou Kane (b. 1928) wrote one major, slightly autobiographical novel, *Ambiguous Adventure* (1961), in which the protagonist, a boy from a pious elite Torodbe family of the Futa Toro, experiences the contradictory effects of a Parisian university education. Ousmane Sembène (1923–2007), by contrast, was a prolific writer and a major film director as well. The son of a Wolof fisherman from the Casamance, Sembène worked as a laborer in the port of Dakar and then in an automobile assembly plant in France. He was largely self-taught, and his first novels, *The Black Dock-Worker* (1956), *Oh Country, My Beautiful People* (1957), and *God's Bits of Wood* (1962), deal directly with the political and social issues he had personally experienced: colonial racism and the exploitation of workers. His later novels, *The Harmattan* (1964) and *The Last of the Empire* (1981), were even more political in content and amounted to a strong critique of the path postindependence African leaders were following.

Beyond his many novels, Ousmane Sembène is remembered as a great filmmaker; he has been designated the "father of African cinema" on more than one occasion. Sembène was keenly aware of the limited relevance of his French-language novels given the depth of illiteracy in Senegal. He thus turned to cinema in 1963, producing *Borom Saret,* a film about a day in the life of a horse and buggy for rent in Dakar's poor Médina neighborhood. Poverty and the political oppression of the poor are dealt with in his subsequent films. *La noire de . . . (So-and-so's Black Girl,* 1966) is a critical look at neocolonialism through the eyes of a Senegalese housemaid in the employ of a French couple; *Manda-bi (The Money Order,* 1968) exposes petty bureaucratic corruption; and *Xala (Impotence,* 1974) explores greed and social irresponsibility. Sembène later turned to Senegal's history for material. *Emitai* (1971) looks at the resistance of the Diola of the Casamance to colonial authority, while *Ceddo* (1977) deals with the struggle between the warrior aristocracy and the Muslim clerics. The important role of women as historical agents is highlighted in both films. *Camp de Thiaroye* (1987) recounts the 1944 mutiny of African troops stationed in Thiaroye, near Dakar. With the political satire *Guelwaar* (1992), Sembène returned to a critique of current neocolonialism. Sembène pioneered grassroots cinema in Africa. He employed nonprofessional actors and distributed his films by touring the countryside himself, setting up his screen and projector on village squares at night.

In the 1980s a new, postindependence generation of authors, novelists, playwrights, and poets began to emerge. The best known of these are women: Mariama Ba and Aminata Sow Fall. In her two novels, *So Long a Letter* (1979) and *Scarlet Song* (1981), Mariama Ba (1921–1981) deals directly and critically with the status of women within both African and Islamic tradition, especially with regard to polygamy. Ba was also an active feminist and wrote a number of essays before her untimely death in 1981. Aminata Sow Fall (b. 1941), on the other hand, has tackled a broad range of contemporary social issues, including poverty, the caste system, and corruption. Her first novel to earn critical acclaim was *The Beggars' Strike or the Dregs of Humanity* (1979), which recounts the deportation of Dakar's street beggars by an ambitious politician. *The Call of the Arenas* (1982) tells of an alienated youth finding himself in traditional wrestling, an activity considered beneath his status by his family. Sow Fall, who continues to publish novels (as well as an essay on Senegalese cuisine, with recipes), is also engaged in promoting culture and literature. Since 1985 she has directed the Centre Africain d'Animation et d'Echanges Culturels and the Khoudia publishing house, both based in Dakar. Other Senegalese women authors include the novelists Nafissatou Diallo (1941–1981) and Myriam Warner Vieyra (b. 1939), and poets Kiné Kirama Fall (b. 1934) and Fatou Ndiaye Sow (1956–2004). Most contemporary Senegalese literature is published by *Nouvelles éditions africaines* in Dakar, though some is published in Paris, by *Présence africaine* or major French publishing houses.

Senegal has a strong, though relatively young, theater tradition. It is mostly in French but sometimes in national languages as well. Like their novelist and poet counterparts, playwrights turn to traditional cultural forms for inspiration: dance, griot tales, folklore, use of masks, religious rituals, and so forth. The best-known contemporary Senegalese playwrights are Cheikh Aliou Ndao (b. 1933), Alioune Badara Béye (b. 1945), Ibrahima Sall (b. 1949), and Marouba Fall (b. 1950). Historical drama is the dominant genre. The most frequently produced Senegalese plays are Cheikh Aliou Ndao's *L'éxile d'Alboury* (1965) and Amadou Cissé Dia's *Les derniers jours de Lat Dior* (1965). Both plays deal with heroic kings who ultimately have to face defeat by the French. The playwright Marouba Fall also writes poetry, where, among other themes, he explores God through classical Sufi tropes: love for the Beloved, friendship, and separation. Another contemporary poet, Amadou Lamine Sall (b. 1951), also explores love, but in a decidedly more profane mode: the "beloved" here standing in for humanity and the planet. Stage productions in Senegal are limited by the lack of resources: few theaters or viable acting troupes, too little funding. The state-run Théâtre Daniel Sorano in Dakar, created in 1965 by President Senghor, is the country's largest and most well-known theater.

Closely related to theater is dance. Practiced in homes, village squares, and street corners, and by women especially, dance is part of the fabric of everyday life in Senegal. Its institutionalized form on stage owes much to this popular practice. Senegal's National Ballet was one of the first cultural institutions set up by President Senghor following independence—part of his project to bring African art into the "Civilization of the Universal" he hoped would replace Western imperialism. The National Ballet produces works that are original, drawing extensively from Senegal's diverse regional dance traditions. The company has toured the world acting as a cultural ambassador for the country. It is perhaps better known abroad than within Senegal. Other Senegalese ballet troops include Mudra Afrique (1977–1983), set up in collaboration with famed French choreographer Maurice Béjart (1927–2007,

Béjart's father, the French philosopher Gaston Berger [1896–1960], lived in Saint Louis). Its first director was the Franco-Beninese choreographer Germaine Acogny (b. 1944), who later founded the Compagnie Jant-bi dance troupe and greatly contributed to the teaching of dance at the Ecole des Sables in Toubab Dialaw. As with theater, there are few resources allocated to dance by the government (outside of the National Ballet) and little private-sector support.

THE PRINT AND BROADCAST MEDIA

Nowhere is French cultural influence stronger today than in the mass media. Not only is French the dominant language of Senegalese print media, but all the major French newspapers and magazines are distributed in Senegal, where they are avidly read by the largely French-educated urban elite. Moreover, French TV programs, accessible with a satellite dish, are widely watched. However, Arabic-language satellite channels from the Middle East are gaining in popularity.

That said, the national Senegalese media are dynamic in their own right. Print journalism has a long history, having thrived in Saint Louis and Dakar during the colonial period; the first Senegalese newspaper, *Le Reveil,* was published in Saint Louis in 1885. Many of the newspapers of the time were affiliated to a particular political party, a feature that continued to characterize the Senegalese press until the 1970s. And while the state exercised a monopoly on radio and TV broadcasting in the first three decades after independence, recent liberalization of the communications sector has led to a burgeoning of private channels. Contrary to the press, these broadcast media operate largely in Wolof and other national languages.

Senegal has five daily newspapers, all based in Dakar. *Le Soleil,* the oldest, was originally government owned but has recently been partly privatized. It was established in 1970 as a successor to *Paris-Dakar* (1933–1961) and *Dakar Matin* (1961–1970). Until the election of Abdouaye Wade to the presidency in 2000, *Le Soleil* also served as an organ for the ruling Parti Socialist. *Sud Quotidien* and *Wal Fadjri* are private newspapers that were set up in the early 1990s by journalists with close ties to Sufi orders: *Sud Quotidien* (originally *Sud Hebdo,* as it was a weekly) by Mourides and *Wal Fadjri* (also originally a weekly) by Tijanis from Kaolack. Their Islamic roots by no means qualify these newspapers as Islamist. Both operate within the liberal tradition of criticizing whichever government is in power. *Le Quotidien,* another private daily, was created in 2003 by a group of lawyers and professionals associated with a media group called Avenir Communication, while *l'Observateur* belongs to a media group called Futurs Média.

In addition to these serious dailies, there are a number of thinner eight-page tabloids, such as *L'Actuel, Le Populaire,* and *Express News,* that allot as much space to the coverage of sports as they do to current political affairs. There is also a genre of political satire comic strips that are occasionally published. The comic strips are interesting in that the narrative text is in French but the cartoon characters speak in Wolof. Another print media genre consists of women's magazines, which appear on a weekly or monthly basis. They cover fashion, the social agenda, and the lives of celebrities, but they also include other topics important to women, such as health and legal issues.

Perhaps in keeping with the French culture in which it is rooted, Senegalese politics revolves around "affairs," that is, political scandals of one type or another but usually involving embezzled funds, a murder, a government minister, opposition leaders, and a court case. These affairs make headlines for weeks or months on end and are avidly followed by a much-politicized reading public. Newspapers and magazines thus play an important role in Senegal's public sphere.

There is an expanding range of options in Senegal's broadcast media. Following independence, the government took control of the airwaves, operating only one radio and TV station, Radio-Télévision du Sénégal (RTS). Political liberalization in the 1990s loosened the government's grip and opened the field to competition. The private commercial-print press was the first to successfully apply for radio broadcast licenses. In 1994 Sud FM (part of the Sud Quotidien group) and WalFM (part of the Walf Fadjri group) opened radio stations first in Dakar and then later in some of the larger regional capitals such as Kaolack and Ziguinchor. Radio Futurs Médias (Futurs Média group) followed suit. In the face of this unprecedented competition, government-owned RTS opened regional radio stations across Senegal.

Even more interesting has been the development of community-based radio stations. Radio Penc Mi, a community radio station aimed at farmers, began broadcasting from the Agricultural Institute in Bambey in 1996, while Radio Oxy-Jeunes began broadcasting from Pikine, Dakar's sprawling working-class suburb, in 1999. Associations affiliated with Sufi orders also obtained licenses; by the beginning of the present decade several Mouride stations were broadcasting from the autonomous holy city of Touba.

The liberalization of TV broadcasting has been more cautious than that of radio. RTS2, the second national TV channel, was privatized in the early 2000s. Several French and South African media groups have obtained licenses to operate TV stations, and a 24-hour Senegalese news channel went on the air in 2006. People who can afford it buy satellite dishes and receivers and access the hundreds of channels available, uncensored, from European (French) and Middle Eastern (Arabic) satellite TV providers.

The effect of the growth of a diverse range of radio and TV channels over the past decade has been immense. The new channels broadcast mostly in Wolof, Pulaar, Sereer, and other national languages, bringing information and entertainment much closer to the people. Apart from the ubiquitous pop music, programming includes health topics (including traditional healing practices once considered taboo), political satire, talk shows with invited guests (often local politicians or officials), current affairs, and live broadcasts from cultural, sports, and political events. Also, the fact that radio stations are now local institutions, based in cities, neighborhoods, and villages across the country, has fostered local accountability. Local officials, elected or otherwise, have been confronted with local public opinion as never before. In Touba, which is run autonomously by the Mouride order, the caliph general of the Mourides shut down the three local radio stations when comments critical of the municipal administration were aired. National and local government officials do not have this option and have had to deal with the increased media scrutiny of public affairs. Though journalists can still find themselves in court, and stations can have their licenses temporarily suspended by the governing regulating board, the free independent press in Senegal is healthy and getting stronger.

The broad diffusion of cell phone and Internet use over the past decade has been equally revolutionary in its effects on society. Previously, telephone land lines were an expensive luxury. Many villages did not have a single phone. In others, one telephone in the general store or medical dispensary served the entire locality. Even in cities, in households wealthy enough to own a telephone, phone use was expensive and restricted. Cell phones have transformed this landscape. As the *Groupe Spéciale Mobile* (GSM) networks of rival providers expand, few villages will be out of range. As for Internet use, though access to personal computers remains a luxury, and in any case limited to the literate, cyber cafés have sprung up all over the country, including in village schools lucky enough to have electricity and an international donor. Moreover, Dakar has strategic access to the undersea fiber optic cable network that encircles the African continent and connects it to Europe and South America. Senegal thus has great potential for growth along the information superhighway. The recent emergence of a customer service call center sector in Dakar may be the first tangible manifestation of this.

ACADEMICS AND SCIENTIFIC RESEARCH

Senegal has a solid institutional framework for scholarship and research. The University of Dakar, now called Université Cheikh Anta Diop, dates from the 1950s, when several colonial-era institutions of higher education were amalgamated. A second university, Université Gaston Berger, opened in Saint Louis in 1990, but Dakar remains the premier hub of research and scholarship. Several major research institutes are located there: the Institut Fondamental d'Afrique Noire (or IFAN; originally called the Institut Français d'Afrique Noire, it changed its name but kept its acronym after independence), affiliated with the university; the West African Research Center (WARC), which operates in English; and the CODESRIA (the Council for the Development of Social Science Research in Africa), a pan-African research center established in 1973. All three institutions are located near the university. Much Senegalese social science scholarship is published in France, by major Africanist publishers such as Karthala and L'Harmattan, as well as by specialized academic presses. However, an increasing number of Senegalese scholars now publish in English, through U.S. academic publishers.

In addition to scientific research, a great many development NGOs operate in Senegal. ENDA-Tiers Monde, created in 1972, is a major international NGO committed to "environment, development, action" throughout the Third World. Its head office is in Dakar. Foreign-based NGOs such as the Canadian government–funded IDRC (International Development and Research Center) and numerous European and European Union NGOs, USAID and the Peace Corps, Christian and Muslim charities, and so forth, are also active. All in all, there are over 500 registered NGOs operating in Senegal. Some are international, but others are national or even locally based. They are active in virtually every sector: gender equality and women's empowerment, sustainable rural and urban development, human rights, children's rights, health care, education, technology transfer, democratization, and so forth. They work closely with other civil society organizations and have become part of the fabric of life for many people.

The multifarious interactions of academics, scholars, writers, artists, journalists, and NGO professionals make Dakar one of Africa's premier intellectual centers, a major hub with links to Europe and North America and across Africa and the Muslim world.

4

Art and Architecture

ART IN SENEGAL is not easily compartmentalized or defined in Western terms. Visual and plastic arts, music, and dance are part of everyday life. They are quotidian acts not separate from work, play, family, business, politics, or religion. There is no clear threshold between this "art of everyday" and formalized art such as paintings, sculptures, theater, music, and architecture professionally produced for consumption. Moreover, much formalized art is created for the tourist market, adding yet another layer of complexity to any description or explanation of it.

STREET ART

The art of everyday life is best experienced at street level. Senegal's streetscapes are visual feasts; murals adorn businesses, homes, mosques, schools, buses, and trucks. The fronts of telephone shops, butcher shops, fast-food snack bars, and sidewalk barbershops can be completely done over in painted murals whose purpose extends well beyond the need for advertisement and signage.

Most murals have a religious theme and relate quite specifically to one of the Sufi orders. The most common representations are portraits of Sheikh Ahmadou Bamba Mbacké, Seydina Issa Laye, Al Hajj Malick Sy, Sheikh Ibra Fall, or others from Senegal's pantheon of Muslim "saints." These hand-painted depictions are iconic—each has a standardized form derived from an original historical photograph—and they serve a number of purposes. Primarily, the image of a holy man on a building or a vehicle identifies the owner as a member of a specific Sufi order, or a specific subbranch of the order affiliated to one particular sheikh or another. In the absence of an image, an inscription serves the same purpose. "Lamp Fall" or "Dabakh" painted on a bus, for instance, is sufficient to identify the owner as a *taalibe* of Sheikh Ibra Fall or Al Hajj Abdoul Aziz Sy, respectively. The image of a saint also brings *baraka,* or "God's blessings," to the premises. This is especially true when the image is accompanied by a religious inscription in Arabic or Wolofal. Typical inscriptions include phrases like *al-hamdu li-llâh* (praise God) and *jeer-jëf Sëriñ Touba* (thank you, sheikh of Touba). There are few small or medium-sized businesses in Senegal that do not display such images and inscriptions. The Sufi religious identification even extends to the choice of name. For instance, the owner of Salon Mame Diarra hasn't put her own name on the hairdressing salon; she has placed the salon in the spiritual care of Mame Diarra Bousso, Ahmadou Bamba Mbacké's saintly mother.

Religious identity and spiritual protection extend inside buildings as well. The living room in a home, where visitors are received, may contain a portrait of the head of household's deceased father. Additionally, there is likely to be a photo of his sheikh hanging on the wall. The portraits on wall calendars and desk mats in offices also clearly identify the Sufi affiliation of their occupants. In fact, pocket-size photos of sheikhs, deceased and living, are hung around the neck as pendants, pinned to caps, or embossed on schoolbags.

Not all murals are religious in content. When murals decorate streets, public fountains, tree trunks, and schoolyards, the content is usually didactic, reminding passers-by not to waste water, telling children to play safely, warning against the dangers of drug use, and so forth. This type of mural proliferated in September 1990 with the Set Setal movement. After torrential rains turned Dakar's streets into stinking quagmires, the city's young people realized that public authorities were either unable or unwilling to clean up the mess, and they took the task of cleaning up (*set setal*) upon themselves. They collected garbage and swept the streets and sidewalks. Moreover, these young people painted the dirty, peeling walls, transforming them into colorful murals. They also modeled discarded metal and wooden objects into impromptu monuments at street intersections, which they renamed. Art was central to the festive and spontaneous nature of the Set Setal movement. The murals created by the youths dealt with social and political themes such as corruption, health, education, and good neighborliness. They also glorified iconic heroes, with Che Guevara sharing wall space with depictions of Bob Marley, Ahmadou Bamba, and the Statue of Liberty.

While for the most part Dakar's street artists have remained anonymous, some, such as Tafaa Seck, Pape Diop, and Pape Mamadou Samb (better known as

Papisto Boy), have established reputations. Papisto Boy prefers the very long, blank walls of the city's industrial neighborhoods. These give him the scope for large, complex figural compositions that juxtapose Senegalese figures like Senghor and Ahmadou Bamba with figures of African empowerment and Third World liberation: Bob Marley, Nelson Mandela, Kwame Nkrumah, Malcolm X, and so forth. Papisto's large compositions are continually being transformed as the artist updates them according to current events. The municipal authorities, however, are not as enthralled with such artwork. Briefly shamed into tolerating the spontaneous street art of Set Setal, they nonetheless view these murals as unauthorized graffiti and occasionally paint over them. In response the French Cultural Center in central Dakar stepped in, authorizing Papisto Boy to use its street-side wall as a canvas for a lively historical composition.

Tourist Art, Sculpture, and Glass Painting

"Tourist art" refers to works produced principally for the tourist market. This category includes works in wood, such as sculptures and masks, and glass paintings.

Senegal does not have the kind of strong sculptural tradition typical of Guinea, southern Mali, or the Ivory Coast, where masks and wooden figures are religious objects. Nonetheless, the country produces such works because tourists expect to find African masks when they visit Africa. A set number of types of these wooden sculptures are produced in sizes that run from "fits in the purse" to "stands on the floor." In addition to a variety of masks, these types include Dogon granary doors, Senufo anthropomorphic statues, and Bamana animal headdresses. Because Senegal does not have the types of hardwood trees necessary for this sculpture, the wood is imported from elsewhere in West Africa. Many of the sculptors working in this sector are from elsewhere, namely, the Ivory Coast and Burkina Faso. The workshops are small, consisting of two or three artists and an apprentice or two. Tall, slender figurines representing a variety of colonial officials are painted in bright colors and mass-produced for tourists, as are the knee-high *jembe* drums, hollowed from a log.

Some of the same techniques used in wood sculpture have been applied to the sculpting of Dakar's volcanic pumice stone. This soft, evenly grained, gray-brown stone is sculpted into human figures or abstract works in outdoor workshops strung along Dakar's Western Corniche, where they are offered for sale to passing motorists.

Sous-verre glass painting constitutes the second major category of tourist art. The *sous-verre* technique requires painting a picture on the reverse side of a pane of glass. Often called "naïve," the flat paintings are very bright, with cartoonish characteristics. *Sous-verre* started out as a popular art form, a folk art produced by artisans for the enjoyment and pious edification of ordinary people. The technique was introduced to Senegal, along with other Muslim devotional literature and apparel, by Lebanese and Moroccan merchants in the late nineteenth century. Originally, religious themes dominated the genre: portraits of Sufi saints, biblical or Koranic scenes like the menagerie on Noah's ark or Al-Buraq, (the Prophet's winged horse), flying over Jerusalem. By the time of independence, artists had begun producing typical scenes—scenes of life in the village, at the market, on the road; street scenes; musicians playing instruments; women dancing; and so forth. National heroes such as Lat Dior and Kocc Barma were also represented. It was at this time that tourists began buying *sous-verre*. The best-known artist of that era was Gora Mbengue (1931–1988). Both changing popular tastes and tourist tastes impacted the themes explored. In the 1970s works included portraits of Bob Marley and Che Guevara, and pan-African and Rastafarian themes and colors were in the forefront. Moreover, formally trained artists such as Germaine Anta Gaye (b. 1953), Sérigne Ndiaye, Abdoulay Thiam, Babacar Ly, and Mamadou Gaye invested in the genre, innovating in both technique and subject matter. No longer exclusively producing street art or tourist art, *sous-verre* artists are now exhibiting in Dakar's top art galleries as well as in galleries in Europe.

STUDIO ART, PAINTING, AND SCULPTURE

Unlike street art or tourist art, studio art is produced by trained artists in studios or workshops, and it is intended for an increasingly international art market. These arts—painting and sculpture especially, but also tapestry—benefited greatly from state patronage during the Senghor years. The First World Festival of Negro Arts, held in Dakar in 1966, was followed by a flurry of state investments in art forms that had not previously been practiced in Senegal. One of the early achievements was the Manufactures Sénegalaises des Arts Décoratifs, set up in Thiès in 1966. It is famous for the large, hand-woven tapestries it produces. Another product of this policy was the creation of an Ecole des Arts in Dakar. The most well-known artists of this generation are Iba Ndiaye (b. 1928), known for his jazz-inspired oil paintings; Papa Ibra Tall (b. 1935), who explored rhythm and African symbolism in painting and tapestry; Alpha Walid Diallo (b. 1927), who, inspired by griot orature, depicted historical events; and Mor Faye (1947–1984), painter of modern, abstract oil paintings. With the managing of Senghor's cultural institutions, these postindependence pioneers were as much government administrators of the art world as they were artists. In both capacities they prepared the field for a second generation of professional artists who have been generally less concerned with Senegalese and African identity and more attuned to global art trends. Viyé Diba (b. 1954), who has a PhD in urban geography, "manufactures" his paintings with locally woven cotton fabrics and recycled materials. He also does sculpture. Sérigne M'Baye Camara (b. 1958) is also both a painter and a sculptor. His work explores the human form across materials. Amadou Khalis Leye paints with construction materials like asphalt, tar, and sand. Moussa Tine (b. 1953) is master at "sculpture paintings," pictorial compositions in relief metal sheet. Moustapha Dimé (1952–1998) specialized in the sculptural reuse of discarded material, including metal and wood jetsam from the ocean.

Senegal's best-known sculptor is Ousmane Sow (b. 1935), a physical therapist by profession who came to art without going to art school. He creates compositions of larger-than-life human figures. His huge composite metal sculptural tableaux include *Nuba Wrestlers* (1988), *The Maasai* (1989), *The Zulu* (1990), *The Peuhl* (1991), *The Battle of Little Bighorn* (1998), and *The Bronzes* (2000). He has also produced public art, creating the *Woman with Flute* sculpture for Dakar's *Porte du Millénaire* monument in 2001 as well as other statues for French cities. Other sculptors include Babacar Sédikh Traoré Diop, who works with stone, and Guibril André Diop and Papa Youssou Ndiaye, who work exclusively with metal.

Currently, Senegal's premier artistic forum is Dakar's biennale, called Dak'Art. First organized in 1990, it aims to advance the works of contemporary African artists, but it also attracts diaspora painters and sculptors from Europe, Asia, and the Americas for a month of exhibits and conferences. The biennale grows in size and scope with each edition. It has outgrown a single venue and is spread out at sites across the breadth of the capital. Moreover, its success has spawned a number of "off" events. Since 2004 organizers of the Dak'Art have published a quarterly arts journal called *Afrik'Arts*. The biennale has had an immense impact on Senegal's art world. It has greatly heightened the visibility of young artists, both domestically and internationally, and it has created an arts forum unique on the continent.

ARCHITECTURE

Senegal's historical and contemporary architecture, while little known outside its borders, is varied and offers a fascinating prism through which to view regional diversity and social dynamics. Distinct regional building traditions, some of them shared with the neighboring countries of Mali and Guinea, still characterize rural architecture today. The Euro-Atlantic architectural tradition of Senegal's coastal settlements links these places to other towns and cities of the Atlantic world. Colonial Dakar was the flagship of the French Empire in Africa and still exhibits a panoply of colonial architectural styles. At the same time, the activities of Senegal's Sufi orders have produced innovative and distinctive contemporary Islamic architecture.

ARCHITECTURE OF THE PRECOLONIAL ERA

As in much of tropical Africa, traditional building practices in Senegal employ relatively perishable materials such as straw, thatch, reeds, wood, and earth. Such buildings do not have long life spans. Families can easily abandon one house and build another. In precolonial times, even the palaces of kings and nobles were built and then abandoned in this fashion. The largely rural precolonial civilization did not consider buildings as heritage, to be preserved and passed on through the generations. Consequently, few examples of traditional architecture from past centuries have survived.

Africa's traditional architecture used to be called primitive, but more recent assessments stress its appropriateness to the climate and environment and its highly developed understanding of building materials. Earthen walls, built of *banco* (sun-dried bricks of mud and straw) or *pisé* (earth that has been rammed into a wooden coffer frame until it sets), offer great thermal insulation, staying cool all day and warm all night. Likewise, thatch roofing is lightweight and insulates the interior from the sun's heat. Both materials necessitate regular maintenance: earthen walls must be resurfaced occasionally, especially after the rainy season, while thatch roofing needs to be replaced when it gets old. The perishable quality of traditional building materials makes them environmentally friendly. They constitute locally available, renewable resources. The introduction of modern materials like cement brick and corrugated sheet-metal roofing has had a negative impact on building traditions and living conditions alike. While these materials are relatively low maintenance compared to earth and thatch, they offer none of the insulating benefits of traditional building materials. Cement and sheet metal houses heat up during the day and are hard to keep warm at night. Moreover, unlike traditional materials, industrial materials are expensive and must be purchased.

In the settled agricultural heartland of the country, the basic housing unit was the compound, an enclosed space that was home to one family—often a large, extended, polygamous household including many generations. A range of small buildings, round or square, often called "huts," were built within the compound. Each wife in a polygamous household had her own house, which had a bedroom, a kitchen area, and storage space. Married sons also had their own houses. Compounds included granaries, hen houses, and livestock pens. Most of the space inside a compound was not built over. It was left open, as many household activities such as cooking, cleaning, eating, child rearing, and entertaining guests occurred outdoors. If the central courtyard did not have a shade tree, a gazebo-like shelter called an *mbaar* was built to provide shade for these activities. Some houses within the compound had covered verandas to give shelter from the sun and the rain. A compound usually had a single door and was isolated from neighboring compounds by open space or at least a narrow footpath; family compounds were rarely built directly against one another.

Settlements consisted of up to about 50 such compounds loosely organized around one or more public squares. While the compound of the village head, local landlord, or senior lineage might have been bigger than the others, and perhaps centrally located within the community, it was not of a different architectural type. Larger settlements were subdivided into separate neighborhoods, or wards, each with its own head. Settlements expanded or contracted as lineages grew or moved away and as old compounds were abandoned for newer ones. The position of a settlement could also shift incrementally over time as old neighborhoods were abandoned and new ones were created a small distance away.

Major regional variations to the previous model exist. In the pastoral areas inhabited by the Peul, settlements were always temporary. Domed tents built of curved wooden ribs, supported by posts and covered by reed mats, were set up wherever was convenient for the grazing of cattle. A household consisted of only one or two such tents, and settlements of only a few households were widely dispersed. When pasture was exhausted, the tents were dismantled and transported to a new site. Where they have settled in permanent villages, the Peul have developed a distinctive mosque design. The perfectly square prayer hall, built of earthen walls, sits within a circular veranda capped by a tall conical thatch roof that gives the building a round appearance from the outside. The most famous mosque of this type was built in Al Hajj Umar Tall's first capital, Dinguiraye, across the border in modern Guinea in 1883. It has recently, unfortunately, been replaced by a cement mosque of conventional design. However, smaller examples of this type of mosque type survive in Bundu and across eastern Senegal.

The traditional Diola house is all in one piece, with up to 15 rooms surrounded by a veranda and capped by a single thatch roof. These *pisé* houses are either square or circular in shape, and the biggest ones have a second floor. The circular houses are doughnut shaped, the center of the round courtyard in the middle of the building being open to sky. Diola villages consist of separate houses of this type strung along embankments above the rice paddies.

The architecture of Toucouleur towns and villages, on the banks of the Senegal River, has much in common, stylistically and technologically, with the well-known Sahelian architecture of Mali's Niger Bend (Timbuktu, Mopti, Jenne, Segou, and the Dogon villages). Toucouleur villages are compact; compounds are contiguous with one another and form streets. Built almost entirely of *banco,* the rectangular buildings have flat roofs and verandas. The facades facing the inner courtyard are decorated with patterned geometric openings—doors, windows, and vents—that let just the right amount of light and air into the interiors. The most distinguished buildings in Toucouleur towns are the mosques. Like the houses, they are built of *banco* and have flat earthen roofs. The rectangular prayer halls are preceded by a screened veranda, also of *banco,* and are surrounded by a thatch-roofed gallery that keeps the sun's rays from reaching the walls of the building. The most famous mosques of this type are in Halwar, first built in the seventeenth century but subsequently rebuilt several times, and in Guédé, also dating from the seventeenth century and now listed as a historic monument. In the absence of such government-sponsored preservation, however, the tendency since the 1980s has been to replace these old *banco* mosques with conventional modern structures built of cement.

The Senegalese government, through the Ministry of Culture, is active in preserving the country's precolonial architectural heritage. Not all of that heritage consists of buildings, however. Trees, too, were important to precolonial settlements, and 13 trees figure on the ministry's list of classified historic sites. Specific trees, baobabs and kapok trees mostly, served many political, social, and religious functions in precolonial communities. Kings were crowned beneath particular trees. Other trees were places where warriors assembled before going to battle, or were the locus of great assemblies of nobles. Some trees were home to the *tuur,* or patron spirits, or else were used by traditional priests and griots for secret rites. In these cases, the tree trunk might have been used for writing. Baobab trees covered in glyphs consisting of a series of dots, dashes, and lines are a feature of all the ancient and densely settled regions of the country. This writing system has not been deciphered, but these *guy mbind* (baobabs of writing) are still held in great respect. In many communities griots were buried within the trunks of ancient baobab trees. These *guy géwel* (baobabs of griots) are still well known locally, and they are never disturbed.

Yet other trees served for public assemblies, for the resolution of legal disputes, or for discussions and decision making. These are called palaver trees, and there is hardly a village in Senegal that does not have one. Palaver trees, called *pénc* in Wolof, tended to stand in the middle of the public square of a village or neighborhood. They provided a shady place for the elders to spend the day and deal with community business. Larger public assemblies were held on the square during the cooler hours of the late afternoon and evening. Palaver trees thus served as the town halls and courthouses of precolonial

communities. They came to embody the collective constitutions and desti-
nies of their communities and were treated with respect. Today the Senegalese landscape is dotted with these historical trees. Even if the town or village
has disappeared, the monumental palaver tree still stands as a reminder and
physical marker. Senegal's historical royal capitals, places like Mboul, Lambaye, Diakhao, and Kahone, which were the seats of power in its precolonial
kingdoms for many centuries, have many such monumental trees. The most
famous is the Guy Njulli (the "Baobab of Circumcision," listed as a historic
monument) in Kahone, capital of the kingdom of Saloum from the sixteenth
century until 1890. In precolonial times the Guy Njulli was the locus of an
annual festival called the *gàmmu,* during which representatives of all of the
kingdom's provinces renewed their homage to the king during festivities that
lasted for days.

Fadhiout, on the Petite Côte, is Senegal's best-preserved precolonial town.
Fadhiout was the main port of the kingdom of Sine. The town occupies
a small artificial midden-island in a lagoon (the legacy of a Neolithic-era
fishing community). The island is densely occupied, with houses contiguous to one another or separated only by narrow streets. The town square
is dominated by the Baak no Maad, or "King's Baobab." The majority of
the town's inhabitants are Christian, and the parish dates from 1878. The
town's Muslims pray at a mosque at the southern tip of the island. Families
store their grain (millet from fields on the mainland) in separate granaries
built on stilts out in the lagoon. Fadhiout's cemetery, where Christians and
Muslims are buried together, occupies a separate seashell island accessible
by a foot bridge. Other islets in the lagoon, off limits to casual visitors, are
home to some of the *pangool,* or traditional spirits. Now part of the city
of Joal, Fadhiout is a major tourist destination and is listed as a protected
national historic site.

COLONIAL ARCHITECTURE

Senegal's colonial-era architectural heritage begins with the Portuguese and
Lançado traders who lived along the Petite Côte and lower Casamance during the sixteenth century. They are believed to have introduced a house type
characterized by a veranda or porch preceding the door. This house type is
also found in the Cape Verde Islands, the Gulf of Guinea, Brazil, and the
Caribbean and is the earliest material example of Senegal's transatlantic cultural links.

Transatlantic architectural commonalities become clearer during the age
of the slave trade. Houses in Gorée and Saint Louis were built by merchants
for the purpose of trade. They generally had two floors. The ground floor
consisted of a courtyard, storage rooms for goods, a kitchen, and sleeping

quarters for house slaves and domestics. The upper floor was reserved for the merchant's family. It consisted of a covered veranda overlooking the courtyard, which accessed the living and sleeping rooms. The upper floor could also have a balcony on the street side, over the main gate to the house.

The famous "slave house" in Gorée, now a museum and memorial to the slave trade, is a typical example of this type of house. It was built in the 1780s by the Pépin, a Métis family. It is not likely that chattel slaves for export were ever kept in this house, because such in-transit slaves were usually kept penned up out-of-doors elsewhere on the island. Rather, the Pépin were merchants who traded in a variety of commodities: grain, wax and hides, and slaves. The house and the family business were run using the labor of domestic slaves, who lodged on the ground floor.

Saint Louis was bigger than Gorée and supported a greater variety of activities and buildings. By the early nineteenth century the houses of its European and Métis inhabitants had acquired a distinctive urban quality. Neatly aligned along a grid of straight streets, the two-story stone and baked-brick houses were built around a central courtyard. As with the earlier prototype, the ground floor was reserved for commerce and trade. The front onto the street might contain a shop, while the lateral and back sides of the court consisted of storerooms, utility spaces, and lodging for domestics. A covered gallery ran all around the courtyard on the second floor. This gallery accessed the living and sleeping rooms of the proprietor's family. The second-floor rooms facing the street led out to a balcony. Merchants' houses of Saint Louis thus share many architectural features with those of contemporaneous cities across the Atlantic, cities like Havana, New Orleans, and Bahia in Brazil. They were also very expensive to build, as the bricks and roof tiles had to be shipped from France.

The scope of colonial architecture expanded tremendously in the late nineteenth century, with the French imposing rule over the interior. French authorities created a prototypical urban space, called a railroad *escale,* that they disseminated throughout all the economically viable parts of the country. An *escale* was a center for the marketing of agricultural produce, typically peanuts, as well as a base to collect taxes from, and administer justice to, the local population. It consisted of a grid of straight streets that crossed at right angles. At the center was the municipal market, placed a few blocks away from the train station. The blocks surrounding the market were occupied by the two-story trading houses of French firms or Lebanese merchants. Built of a steel frame with brick infill, these buildings could have a balcony above the sidewalk, on the street side. These colonial towns were set up at regular intervals all along the railroads, and much of this turn-of-the-century commercial architecture still stands today, albeit in a rundown state.

Dakar was by far the biggest and most important colonial city in Senegal. In 1902 it became the administrative capital of a federation of colonies extending all the way to Lake Chad. Consequently, significant attention was paid to erecting buildings able to express the power of the colonial authorities. Until the 1930s, the architecture of these official buildings was generically colonial. Administrative or residential buildings were erected according to standard plans found in civil engineering manuals employed right across the tropical colonies of the empire, from Indochina through Africa and on to the Antilles. For perceived hygienic reasons, major public buildings, whether hospitals, barracks, courthouses, or schools, were built as isolated structures in the center of large plots lushly planted with trees and flowers. They were generally two-story structures, with both the ground and upper floor being completely surrounded by verandas intended to shade the walls from direct sun. As much as possible, the rooms inside opened at both ends to ensure maximum cross ventilation. Many of Dakar's surviving older government buildings, such as the Chamber of Commerce and the Ministry of Foreign Affairs (both on Place de l'Indépendence), are of this type. French officials serving in the colony were housed in villas, detached houses with verandas surrounded by gardens. Some of these houses can still be seen in Dakar's Plateau neighborhood.

In the mid-1930s, official architectural policy changed. It was believed that the West African colonies of the empire deserved a style of their own, and the neo-Sudanic style, loosely based on the architectural vocabulary of the historical Malian cities of Jenne and Timbuktu, was adopted for this purpose. The basic plan of the typical colonial building was not altered, but the composition of its facades and ornamentation were changed. Tapering buttresses and pinnacles punctuated the facades and the skyline, as did prominent protruding gargoyles. Highly stylized art deco versions of traditional geometric patterns were incorporated around windows. The Pasteur Institute, the Museum of African Art, the maternity ward of the Dantec Hospital, the Sandaga Market (all located in Dakar's Plateau neighborhood), and the Policlinic in the Médina neighborhood are the best surviving examples of a style whose implementation and diffusion were cut short by World War II. Following the war, the high modern, or international, style dominated official architecture. Good examples of this are the 11-story Administrative Building across the street from the Presidential Palace, built to house a growing civil service, and the National Assembly (Senegal's parliament building), on Soweto Square.

African subjects of the empire did not generally benefit from the colonial architecture. The still largely rural population continued to build according to the traditional practices described at the beginning of the chapter. Senegalese who moved to the new towns along the railroads or to the port cities had to adapt their rural housing tradition to the new environment. Relatively large, nonsanitized plots (having neither running water nor sewer connection) were allocated to Africans by the colonial authorities. The new inhabitants arranged these compounds as they did their village homes, building separate houses with verandas for wives and sons. Much of the space, at least initially, remained unbuilt and was used as an open courtyard for daily chores and activities. Over time, these properties came to be more densely occupied. Dakar's Médina neighborhood started out this way. Though it is now characterized by four-and five-story apartment blocks, some of the original single-family homes of the 1920s and 1930s can still be seen.

Senegal's two historic colonial towns, Gorée and Saint Louis, are on the United Nations Educational, Scientific, and Cultural Organization's (UNESCO) list of World Heritage Sites. They are major tourist destinations and have attracted significant private real estate investments over the past decade or so. Gorée is a tiny island, less than 1 mile in length and only 350 yards at its widest. It is linked to the port of Dakar by regular ferry service (pedestrians only, no cars). The entire island of Gorée serves as a memorial to the inhumanity of the transatlantic slave trade. The "house of slaves," mentioned earlier, serves this purpose, as does a newer commemorative monument at the summit of the southern hill, which overlooks the town. Other monuments include the Catholic Church and the archeological museum, housed in the circular bastion built to defend the little harbor. Most of the island's historic merchants' houses have been restored and converted into hotels, restaurants, and bed-and-breakfasts. Gorée, with only 1,000 permanent residents, has a thriving arts community and regularly hosts music concerts and international events.

Saint Louis, with about 170,000 inhabitants, is a major regional capital. The historic heart of the city lies on a one-and-half-mile long island in the Senegal River. Much of the urban fabric on the island dates back to the nineteenth century. The island's southern ward was home to the city's Métis community, who patronized the Catholic institutions, and the northern half was home to the city's Muslim population and institutions. As Saint Louis was the capital of the colony until 1958, it has many historic public buildings, including the Cathedral, the Colonial Council building, and the sprawling complex of the Gouvernance, which has been home to the governor and his administration since the 1660s. Less evocative of the slave trade than Gorée, Saint Louis is renowned for its exquisite urbanity. The culture of the Métis, and of the *signares* in particular, was both refined and urbane. Public life in the city, on the streets and in the squares, was essential to this culture of elegance and *savoir vivre,* and this tradition lives on in the city's numerous cultural and artistic events.

Saint Louis's urban cultural heritage extends well beyond its colonial-era architecture. It includes a living tradition of street life. The most common, quotidian of public events in Saint Louis is the *takussanu,* an evening stroll through town in which a woman can show off her newest gown and hairdo. It is a time for socializing with neighbors and acquaintances, a time and place to see and to be seen. The *tànn-béer* is an improvised street party, often initiated by a woman who hires a group of musicians. Upon hearing the beat of the *sabar* music, other women in the neighborhood assemble to dance. A *tànn-béer* can be organized on any number of occasions, or for no particular reason at all. The *simb,* on the other hand, is a form of street theater organized only during religious holidays. During a *simb,* an actor, dressed as a ferocious lion and accompanied by musicians, terrorizes children and adults along the street until he is mastered by a spirit medium called the *diakat.* Another street event popular with children is the *taajabóon,* held on the eve of the Muslim New Year. On that night, Saint Louis's children dress up in a mockery of adults and go door-to-door asking for candy. Another nighttime event is the *fanal,* a procession of colored paper lanterns held each year on Christmas Eve. The lanterns are huge; each is either carried by a dozen men or wheeled down the street on a cart. Neighborhoods compete each year to create ever more fantastic shapes. During the 1950s, in the lead-up to independence, the *fanal* was banned by the authorities because it had become a forum for the expression of political grievances. It has since been revived, and it now provides the city with one of its principal tourist events. Another annual event is the regatta on the river. Teams of boatmen from Guet Ndar, Saint Louis's fishing neighborhood on the ocean, expert in handling the pirogue, compete in a number of categories.

ARCHITECTURE OF THE SUFI ORDERS

Not all the architecture during the colonial era was produced by the colonial authorities. This is the period when Senegal's newly founded Sufi orders were beginning to expand and organize activities. They produced monuments, principally mosques and mausolea, that stand out in Senegal's urban landscape today.

Major Islamic monuments are a new phenomenon in Senegal. Prior to colonization, mosques tended to be very small, at least by the standards of the Muslim world at that time, and they adopted vernacular styles and building technologies, as with the Peul and Toucouleur mosques described earlier. With colonization, masonry construction in stone, baked brick, and concrete was introduced to mosque architecture. The first urban mosques, in Saint Louis (built in the northern quarter, 1844–1847) and Dakar (Carnot Street,

1880s), adopted the neo-Gothic architectural style then in vogue for church architecture. Both of these mosques used the Gothic arch for windows and galleries. They also had two minarets on the front facade, flanking an entrance narthex beneath a pediment—just as the entrance to a church is often flanked by twin steeples or bell towers. The left-side minaret of each mosque incorporated a clock. The Rue Carnot Mosque in Dakar has since been enlarged several times, masking these architectural elements, but they are still evident in the Friday Mosque in Saint Louis. Likewise, the Layène mosques in Yoff and Cambérène, on the northern outskirts of Dakar, incorporated Gothic architectural elements. The Cambérène mosque, built in 1937, has Gothic arch windows, and both it and the Yoff-Layène mosque (1925) have a classically proportioned pediment on the front facade, above the main entrance.

In the early twentieth century the Sufi orders embraced modern construction methods such as steel and reinforced concrete, taking mosque construction to a new level. Sheikh Ahmadou Bamba Mbacké built the first of the new monumental mosques in Diourbel during World War I. At that time, Ahmadou Bamba was living in Diourbel under house arrest. Though France was at war with the Ottoman Empire, he had the mosque built according to the Ottoman plan, with a large central dome over the prayer hall and minarets at the four corners. This was the first domed mosque in Senegal. The building of such a monumental mosque under these conditions was significant in several regards. First, it signified the power of the Mouride order, which was able to mobilize sufficient funds and manpower during wartime to erect the structure in only two years. Second, it demonstrated the cultural autonomy of the order, which chose its own architectural style independently of local tradition or French influence. Third, to his followers, it marked a victory of Sheikh Ahmadou Bamba over the colonial system, as even under house arrest he demonstrated that he exercised significant power over people and resources.

The Mourides also built the second monumental mosque in Senegal, the Great Mosque in Touba. Built between 1930 and 1963, the mosque was gigantic (100 × 80 yards) by the standards of that time and place. Colonial authorities thought it was a waste of resources, but they could do nothing to halt construction because the project was entirely funded by the Mouride order. In its completed form, the mosque is distinguished by its unique central minaret, which reaches over 250 feet. The minaret is popularly called Lamp Fall and has acquired iconic status for the Mourides, appearing on countless murals, calendars, sous-verre paintings, storefront signs, and the sides of buses. Like the Diourbel mosque before it, Touba's mosque was considered a wonder and a providential sign of God's grace. Touba was little more than a village at the time of the mosque's construction. Water was scarce. A spur of the railroad, also entirely financed and built by the Mourides, had to be built to the construction site. Yet the Mourides built their mosque despite the impediments of the colonial system, the Great Depression of the 1930s, and World War II. Since its completion in 1963, the mosque has continually been enlarged and embellished, most recently by a new surface covering of imported white and pink marble.

Senegal's other Sufi orders have also produced distinctive architecture. In the 1920s a large pilgrimage hostel was built in the Qâdirî town of Ndiassane. The three-story concrete structure has hundreds of rooms and over a dozen reception halls and is surrounded by screened verandas. Its purpose was to accommodate as many guests as possible of those who congregate in Ndiassane for the annual pilgrimage.

The Tijâniyya during the colonial period had more modest architectural policies. Early on, the Malikiyya branch of the order, based in Tivaouane, had impressive *zâwiyas* built in both Saint Louis and Dakar. What was impressive was not so much their size or style but their location in the heart of the colonial capitals. Since independence, various branches of the Tijâniyya have produced larger monuments. Construction began on the Great Mosque of Madina Baye, in Kaolack, in 1958. The Great Mosque in the autonomous Tijânî city of Madina Gounass was finished in 1970. Both are built of reinforced concrete, and the Madina Baye mosque, like the one in Diourbel, has a large central dome and four corner minarets. Another large domed mosque is currently being built by the Tijânîs of Tivaouane. Construction started in 1984 and continues today.

The most distinctive feature of twentieth-century Sufi architecture in Senegal is the originality of design. While the classical cannons of Islamic architecture—use of arches, domes, and portals—have not been ignored, neither have models from elsewhere in the Muslim world been slavishly copied. For example, Diourbel's mosque was built according to the Ottoman plan, but it looks nothing like a Turkish mosque in terms of style. This independence of design on the part of Senegal's Sufi orders contrasts with the government-funded Great Mosque in Dakar, inaugurated in 1966, which was built entirely in the imported Moroccan style. New, reinforced concrete mosques regularly spring up all over Senegal. The plasticity of form allowed by reinforced concrete is exploited by architects to produce unique minarets and domes, the tall spiral minaret in Tivaouane being the most recent expression of this trend. The Mosque of the Divinity, built on Dakar's Ouakam beach in 1992, is another example of current trends in mosque design. In Touba also, there has been an explosion of mosque construction since the beginning of the millennium. While the architectural style may be eclectic, it is always original.

Senegal's Sufi architecture extends beyond mosque design. The Sufi orders have been very influential on the urbanization process. There are many cases of entire neighborhoods or even cities being designed and built by the orders. The Mouride order in particular has promoted some innovative and well-adapted housing. In Touba and other cities under its jurisdiction it allots very large house plots so that large extended families can continue to thrive in an urban context. Meanwhile, the sheikhs and caliphs of the orders have built palatial compounds in the cities where they reside. The Tijânî sheikhs of Tivaounae and Kaolack live in multistory town houses, while Mouride sheikhs have generally maintained the traditions of the great rural compound. One Mouride sheikh, Sëriñ Omar Sy, built a large compound outside Diourbel entirely of bundles of straw and reeds. Reeds serve to write the Word of God (i.e., the Koran), explains the sheikh, so living in a house of reeds is like living in God's Word.

CONTEMPORARY ARCHITECTURE

Senegal acceded to independence at a time when the international style was hegemonic. This style was considered the epitome of modernity and progress, and Senegal, like other newly independent African countries, embraced it officially. Public buildings built by the new state, such as Dakar's Palais de Justice (built in 1959 but now closed because of structural weaknesses) and the Musée d'Art Dynamique (built in 1966, now the Court of Appeals), adopted this style. Beyond the progressive and international qualities of this style, it was felt that this style was also appropriate to the national and pan-African cultural context. Dakar's first skyscraper, the 25-story head office of the BCEAO (the central West African bank responsible for the common CFA currency), built in 1977–1979, was designed by Pierre Atepa Goudiaby (b. 1947) to resemble the trunk of a baobab, a tree with deep symbolic significance. Once again it is the plasticity of reinforced concrete—that is, the ability of this construction material to take virtually any form—that permits it to express traditional patterns previously produced in earth, wood, and thatch.

For the most part, the architecture of independent Senegal has not been very inspired. The state patronage of the first two decades, when new public buildings were needed, dwindled during the structural adjustment era of the 1980s and 1990s. Currently, government planners in Dakar are dreaming of a Dubai-type skyline. President Wade has announced the intention of moving the city's international airport to a new location and developing the old site as an international business center, with a phalanx of gleaming steel-and-glass skyscrapers. But so far, private investors have not been eager to spend on flashy architecture. It seems that only mosque-building is deemed important enough to warrant the expense. The wealthy certainly spend money on their gated private homes, but for most people, architecture is about housing the family as best they can with the resources they have.

DOMESTIC SPACE AND FURNISHINGS

Apart from apartment units in the centers of cities, which account for a growing category of urban housing, most Senegalese homes are single-family units centered on a courtyard. The courtyard is "women's space" to the extent that it is where most housework—cooking, cleaning, and child rearing—is performed. Yet gender segregation in the house, between a private "off-limits" harem and a more "public" front accessible to male guests, which is characteristic of many parts of the Muslim world, is not commonly practiced in Senegal outside the Sufi elite. Women habitually perform housework out on the street in front of the house, in full view of passers-by. Both the courtyard and the street front are kept clean, being swept daily. In villages, the courtyard is also used for farmwork such as the husking of millet and the raising of foul. In cities, the courtyard is likely to be tiled over, with a drain for water.

Various buildings face the courtyard. They generally date from different periods, as the family compound has developed over the decades according to need. The oldest house usually faces the main door of the compound across the courtyard. It has a covered gallery, screened from the sun, that accesses a central living room. Two lateral rooms, one at each end of the gallery, are the bedrooms of the original heads of household, the husband and the first wife. The kitchen is often a separate little house containing a hearth for rainy days; otherwise, the cooking is done outside in a corner of the courtyard. Each subsequent wife in a polygamous household will have her own house facing the courtyard. It may be smaller than the first house, with only one or two rooms off the gallery. Children do not have rooms of their own. Younger ones sleep with their mothers or sleep in the living room. Only when several children are old enough will a new house with rooms for them be built on another spot around the courtyard. All the buildings in the compound are one room deep, meaning each room has a window or door at opposite ends to ensure maximum ventilation—air conditioning is a luxury most Senegalese cannot afford. These openings in the masonry are designed to keep the heat, dust, and direct sunlight out of the rooms.

Of course, denser urban areas do not allow for such flexibility in occupancy. Today's real estate market provides Western-style villas, detached single-family homes with a surrounding garden and a carport. These houses are designed like any Western bungalow, except the cooking and cleaning are still likely to take place outside, on the terrace next to the kitchen at the back of the house. Housing units in modern apartment blocks resemble similar units found elsewhere around the world.

In keeping with the modest means of most Senegalese families, house furnishings are minimal: a few beds (kids sleep on foam mattresses that are easily stored), a few wooden stools, and a chest of drawers or a clothes cabinet. Mats, of reeds or plastic fiber, are an important furnishing. They are set out in the shade, on a veranda or in the courtyard, and easily moved about throughout the day as the sun crosses the sky. Meals are typically taken on a mat. A large enamel-coated dish is set in the middle, and family members squat around to eat. People sit or recline on mats to relax or perform a household task. Guests are received by the host seated on a mat. Bedrooms can also be used for receiving guests. Both men and women receive visitors seated on their beds. Women keep their kitchen utensils, including multiple sets of enamelware pots from China, in their rooms, where they are displayed. Incense, brought in on earthen charcoal-burning braziers, is burned in the rooms to create a pleasing ambience for guests. Decoration inside the house consists mostly of framed photographs of older family members and religious pictures (photos of Sufi sheikhs, images of Mecca or the prophet Muhammad's tomb in Medina). Refrigerators, TVs, and radio-CD players are common household appliances, but personal computers, dishwashers, and washing machines are not.

Access to affordable housing is a critical issue in Senegal. Senegal's population is still growing at the high rate of about 2.5 percent per year, and rural-urban migration is bringing more and more people to the cities—to the greater Dakar metropolitan region in particular. Despite a host of publicly funded housing programs, backed by international organizations and NGOs, the housing needs of the poor are still not being met. This inability to provide housing for those who need it has contributed to the growth of shantytowns. Though it is difficult to quantify, some estimate that 30 percent of Dakar's population, nearly 1 million people, lives in shantytowns such as Diamaguen and Yeumbeul. Inhabitants of these neighborhoods come mostly from villages, bringing their rural lifestyle with them. Shantytown dwellers must commute long distances to reach potential revenue-producing activities, as shantytowns are built on the outskirts of the city.

Shantytowns get their name from the precarious and flimsy nature of their construction materials: metal sheeting, plastic sheets, cardboard, recycled planks, and so forth. Over time, however, shantytowns "harden." As residents earn money, they rebuild their houses in cement and other more permanent material. They also add floors and hook up electricity. No longer composed of shanties, these slum neighborhoods are called "irregular," "spontaneous," or "under-equipped." They have only a skeletal water distribution system through a few public fountains, no sewage system, and only a precarious connection to the electricity grid. They are also deficient in schools and health centers. Yet shantytowns and slums are not entirely hopeless manifestations of urbanity. Shantytown dwellers are organized in associations, led mainly by women, which have successfully lobbied for better public services. Shantytown women have also set up their own microbusinesses. One such business is peri-urban agriculture, in which vegetables are grown on tiny irrigated plots and then taken into the city and sold.

Senegal is home to an ancient rural civilization. More than 50 percent of its population lives in villages. Village life inspires much of its contemporary culture and art.

For the Peul, cattle are not just an economic asset. They are essential to social relations and collective identity.

The "Baobab of Circumcision" in Kahone, capital of the kingdom of Saloum for many centuries, is listed as a national monument. It was the scene of an annual civic festival called the gàmmu, where nobles and warriors from every province assembled to renew their allegiance to the king. Similar historic trees dot the Senegalese landscape.

Well beyond simply serving the needs of transportation and circulation, streets are central to community life. Life-cycle events such as baptisms and weddings are celebrated not only with family and friends but with the whole neighborhood. In this scene a tent and chairs have been set up in the street and finger food is being prepared for the guests, who will arrive later in the afternoon.

Special architectural care is lavished on mosques and the public spaces surrounding them. Santhiaba Mosque in Dakar's Medina neighborhood, pictured here, is important to the Lebu community. Here, the mosque square also harbors a monumental baobab tree, which is equally well tended.

Religion infuses business culture. The commercial artwork on this upholsterer's shop in Cambérène (near Dakar) clearly identifies its owner as a member of the Layène Sufi order. The images of Seydina Issa Rohou and Mame Alassane Laye, two former caliphs of the Layène, also help place this business under divine protection.

Urban youth, in Dakar in particular, have taken to decorating the walls of houses and businesses with colorful painted murals. The painting at this public fountain in Dakar's Medina neighborhood depicts a woman at a village well.

Sous-verre paintings on display on one of Dakar's main streets.

The market is women's space. Women are both the sellers and the buyers of fruit, vegetables, and condiments. They also run the lucrative and diverse retail trade in cloth.

Sheep for sale in the lead-up to the Tabaski holiday.

The boys in this *daara* (school) in Touba are using wooden boards and washable ink to help memorize the Koran. Such Koranic schooling constitutes the only formal education many children receive.

Old-fashioned, do-it-yourself toys still bring glee to children. These three boys entertain themselves by racing hoops down a street.

Hairdos are important to the personal expression of women of all ages. A young woman braids her little sister's hair into tight cornrows (*above left*). An advertisement for hair extensions (*above right*), hung in a cosmetics shop, displays typical fashions for young women.

Posters of heavyweight wrestling champions adorn the wall of a store.

5

Cuisine and Traditional Dress

Staple Foods, Meats, Vegetables, and Fruit

TODAY'S SENEGALESE DIET is based on rice and bread, but this has not always been the case. Both white rice and white flour for bread are dietary innovations of the colonial period, and both foods must be imported to meet today's consumer demand. Historically, the staple cereals of the Senegalese diet have been millet and sorghum, which come in several varieties: *suuna, saaño, basi, njaxnaat,* and *tiñ.* These cereals are too coarse to make good flour. Consequently, they are consumed as porridge. Ground millet can be "rolled" by hand to form couscous, a tiny form of pasta, which is then boiled or steamed. Pulses, or beans (*ñebbe*), and cow's milk complement these staple cereals.

While millet and sorghum are still consumed, especially in the villages where they are produced, Senegalese cuisine has adopted white rice. An African variety of rice has long been grown in the lower Casamance, and its production is essential to Diola culture and identity. But it has never been produced as a market crop, and the quantity produced in that region could not begin to meet the requirements of national consumption. Neither can the modern irrigated rice perimeters of Richard Toll, in the lower Senegal Valley. Most of Senegal's rice is imported from South and Southeast Asia.

Vegetables are an important element of Senegalese cuisine. Senegal produces a great variety of vegetables, including tubers such as potatoes, sweet potatoes, turnips, carrots, and yams, as well as onions, cabbage, peppers, and various squashes and eggplant. Most are available year round. A variety of fruit, such as melons (*xaal*), mangos, oranges, and limes, is also available, but this depends far more on the seasons. Much fruit cultivation occurs in the *niayes,* the humid inter-dunar depressions along the coast north of Dakar. The main condiments used in Senegalese cooking are gumbo, hot pepper, ginger, tamarind leaves, and baobab fruit.

Most animal protein in the Senegalese diet comes from fish. The most common species consumed are the white grouper, the bluespotted sea bream, the red pandora, the West African goatfish, the African threadfin, and various species of croaker. Fresh fish is available daily in markets along the coast, but in the absence of affordable refrigeration technologies, inland markets deal mainly with dried fish—the freshly caught fish being dried on beaches as soon as it comes ashore.

Meat is a luxury for most household budgets and is consumed only on special occasions such as family events and religious festivals. Special dishes, many of them sweet, are prepared for the three days of socializing and feasting that follow Korite, which marks the end of the holy fasting month of Ramadan. Tabaski, which marks the culmination of the *hajj* pilgrimage in Mecca, requires every household to sacrifice a sheep. Grilled mouton is thus prepared in a variety of ways in the following days. Cow's milk is consumed fresh or curdled (*kàcc meew*), sometimes sweetened and added to porridge (*laax*), but cheese and yogurt are not traditional dairy products.

The traditional cooking oil in Senegal used to be shea butter (*kaarite*), derived from the seeds of the shea tree. However, since Senegal began producing peanuts in the nineteenth century, peanut oil has been used for most cooking.

Cuisine

Lunch is the main meal in Senegal, and it usually consists of a rice dish. Breakfast is light: a French-style baguette (wheat does not grow in Senegal; the flour is imported) with butter (also imported from Europe) and coffee or tea. Dinner is a hot meal, but still lighter than lunch. It might consist of a noodle dish or an omelet, with bread. Both lunch and dinner are taken collectively. The meal is presented in a single large dish or bowl, which is set in the middle of a mat on the floor. People then squat around it to eat. In traditional table etiquette, people eat with the fingers of the right hand, making a little ball of food to be popped into the mouth. Nowadays, though, soup spoons are commonly used. In large families, and in more conservative Muslim families, men eat separately from the women and children. Among the men, eating is a serious, almost religious, affair. Every meal begins with the *basmallah,* or "thanks to God." There is no idle banter. A short word about how delicious the food is suffices. Among the women, who must feed the children, the meal is more convivial. Discussion and laughter are allowed. Among urban, middle- and upper-class families, Western meal etiquette now rules. Meals are taken together, seated at a table, with individual plates and cutlery.

Senegal's national dish is rice and fish, or *cebbu jën.* The rice, which must first be rinsed profusely in cold water to remove the starch, is cooked in a light tomato sauce. Dried fish is then stuffed with a mixture of parsley, red pepper, and *bisaab* (hibiscus leaf) and slowly grilled or fried. The stuffed fish is placed on a bed of the tomato rice along with onions, carrots, cabbage, gumbo, eggplant, turnips, and yams, which have also been stewing in the tomato sauce. Condiments and seasoning include hot red pepper and tamarind. Rice and fish is the best-loved dish in Senegal. Most families eat some variant of it for lunch most days of the week. It is also popular abroad, throughout western Africa, Europe, and North America, where Senegalese have settled and opened restaurants. Its status as the national dish is thus well deserved.

Two other rice dishes, *yaasa* and *maafe,* rank just behind *cebbu jën* in terms of popularity. *Yaasa* is a marinated dish usually prepared with chicken, but it can also be prepared with fish. First a marinade of lemon juice, vinegar, onions, and mustard is prepared; pitted olives can also be added. A dismembered chicken must marinate in this preparation, preferably overnight. Pieces of chicken are removed from the marinade and browned. The remaining marinade, consisting of onions mostly, is then fried in oil. Water and spices such as ginger, thyme, and hot red pepper are added to make a sauce. The chicken then simmers in the sauce. The chicken *yaasa* is presented on a bed of white rice.

Maafe is a beef dish prepared in a peanut sauce, though chicken or lamb can also be used. Beef cubes are sautéed in a ginger and onion sauce. Tomato paste, water, and an assortment of cut vegetables are then added to make a stew. When the beef and vegetables are nearly cooked, peanut butter (unsalted and unsweetened) is stirred in. The *maafe* then simmers some more. Like *yassa,* it is served on a bed of white rice. Because they usually use relatively expensive meat and poultry rather than fish, *yaasa* and *maafe* are festive dishes prepared only on special occasions.

BEVERAGES

Festive occasions also call for the serving of refreshing drinks. *Bisaab* is made from hibiscus leaves, whose acidity makes it tangy. *Jinjéer,* as the name implies, is made from crushed ginger. Both *bisaab* and *jinjéer* are served cold and sweet. The mixture of cold, sweet, and powerfully tangy makes these drinks particularly refreshing, and they are holding their ground in the face of the ongoing onslaught of industrial bottled soft drinks.

Also holding its own is the traditional tea service. Tea (*àttaaya*) is the social drink of preference in Senegal. It is served on many different occasions— in the intimacy of a quiet afternoon, at work, when guests arrive, and so forth—and it involves elaborate preparation. Tea is served in three "acts," called *loowel, ñaari,* and *ñetti* (first, second, third). The first service is the strongest. Green tea leaves (imported) boil in the teapot along with some sugar. After the first service, the same leaves are boiled again, and more sugar is added. The second service is thus weaker, but sweeter, than the first. The third service is the sweetest, and mint leaves are added at the last moment to scent it. Tea is served in small glasses that have been carefully prepared before each service. Froth is created in each glass by pouring a bit of the sweetened tea from one to the other over and over again from a certain height. The entire three-act tea service can take up to two hours. Often it is the youngest male present who is assigned the task of preparing tea.

A distinctive coffee, called café touba, has become very popular over the past decade. As its name implies, café touba was first developed in Touba, the Mouride holy city. The coffee plant does not grow in Senegal; it grows far- ther south, in Guinea and the Ivory Coast. Until the 1980s, most Senegalese drank only instant coffee. Guinean coffee beans then started to be imported into Touba, where they were mixed with the ground beans of the *jaar* tree. The resulting café touba, drunk sweet with condensed milk, has a unique, spicy kick found in no other drink. It is served for breakfast or in the after- noon and is also available at sidewalk food stands in cities across Senegal. It is also now marketed in Europe and North America, wherever Mourides live. The distinctive drink has become emblematic of the recently acquired global reach of the Mouride order.

Another stimulant, more traditional and with a longer presence in Senegal, is the nut of the kola tree. The cola nut, one of the main ingredients in Coca Cola, grows in the wetter forested countries to the south of Senegal, but cola nuts have been traded north and consumed in Senegal for many centuries. Cola nuts are among the few drugs not expressly prohibited by Islam, hence their widespread popularity in the Muslim countries of West Africa. Hard and bitter, they are bitten into and chewed, usually in the morning hours. The reddish nuts are sold, along with tooth sticks (the traditional form of dental hygiene), by sidewalk vendors.

DRESS, FABRICS, AND CLOTHING

Clothing and fashion are even more important than cuisine to personal and national identity, especially for Senegalese women. Senegalese women project an aristocratic demeanor, expressed in stately stature, elegant clothes, and a refined manner. Some have traced this tradition to the famous *signares* of Saint Louis and Gorée, who set a high standard for subsequent generations of urban women. The concept of *élégance* dates from the *signare* era and has passed into colloquial Wolof. *Elégance* encapsulates the public persona every woman aspires to attain. The importance of maintaining this public demeanor can hardly be overestimated. Women spend a considerable part of their disposable income on fabrics, clothing, hairstyles, accessories, and jewelry, as this is how they express their aspirations and actual social status.

Elégance begins with fabrics. Historically, cloth has been one of the most valued manufactured goods in West Africa, and bolts of cloth were once used as currency. Cloth used to be woven from vegetable fibers obtained from the fruit of kapok trees and from baobab bark, but this is no longer the case. Cotton is the only cloth woven in Senegal today. Weaving used to be the prerogative of the *ràbb* caste, and it is still done almost exclusively by men, though it is women who dominate the trade in cloth. Traditional weaving uses a narrow loom. It produces very long strips of cloth about 8 inches wide, which are sewn together to make bolts that can then be dyed. Because of the space required (the pieces are up to 20 yards long), the work of weaving is often conducted in the street or on the sidewalk. The type of cloth produced in this fashion tends to be coarse, and it is used mostly for men's clothes or for making tapestries. However, because it is homespun and hand woven, strip cloth fetches a high value in the specialty markets of the developed world. Finer cotton strip cloth from Guinea and Guinea Bissau, called *manjak* cloth, is also highly valued by Senegalese women.

Most women's clothing is made from *legoos* (named for Lagos in Nigeria), which is an industrially manufactured thin cotton printed fabric. Senegalese textile factories produce much *legoos*. The cloth is sold in two separate two-yard bolts, called *pagne* in French. One is used to make the wrap-around skirt, which reaches the mid-calf or the ankle. The second *pagne* is used for the matching tunic, which reaches the mid-thigh. Enough of the cloth will be reserved for the headscarf, worn as a turban. This constitutes the everyday "three-piece suit" of Senegalese women.

Legoos are inexpensive fabrics, but their prints are intended to imitate "wax," a much higher-quality batik fabric. Brightly colored batik fabrics first entered the Senegalese market in the seventeenth century, brought from Indonesia by Dutch merchants. Eventually, the Dutch produced batik themselves, for the African market, and "Dutch wax" is still the premier quality batik available in West Africa today. Lesser-quality "London wax" is more affordable than the Dutch variety. The intensity of color obtained by the batik dyeing technique makes printed *legoos* cloth look positively pale in comparison. Wax cloth is used by women of means for the prestigious Western-style dresses, which generally have tight, form-fitting bodices and lots of flounce and lace. What both wax and imitation *legoos* have in common is the continual change in motifs. The fashion industry is driven by the search for novelty; last year's patterns are immediately evident to the discerning eye, and women are thus very keen to wear the latest design.

Mbaseñ (often called *basin* in French) is another popular fabric, used for both women's and men's clothing. Of higher quality than *legoos* but less expensive than wax, *mbaseñ* is a damask characterized by fine textured designs woven into the tight canvas-like cotton. These patterns can be geometric, floral, or pictorial (with Islamic motifs like crescent moons, palm trees, or camels). *Mbaseñ* comes in colors ranging from white to indigo, green, brown, and ochre, but because of its inwoven design, it is not usually printed over. *Mbaseñ* is always used for the confection of *mbubbs* (or *grands boubous* in French). The *boubou,* which both women and men wear, is the traditional outfit worn on special occasions. What distinguishes the woman's three-piece *boubou* from the workaday *legoos* type is that the outer tunic is much more ample. It reaches to the ankles, and its wide, open sleeves can be rolled up to the shoulders. The man's three-piece *boubou* outfit consists of baggy pants, embroidered at the ankles and tied at the waist; a long-sleeved inner tunic that reaches to the thighs and is embroidered around the boat neck; and a very ample over-gown that hangs from the shoulders to the ankles. The three pieces are always cut from the same cloth, and they are always embroidered, usually with gold thread. The man's over-gown in particular has a massive amount of embroidery around the V neck and the breast pocket. More everyday traditional clothing for men consists of a simple caftan, which is a narrow, long-sleeved body-length robe worn over a pair of trousers.

Mbaseñ is also used to make *cuub,* an overdyed or tie-dyed cloth used for women's clothing. The best *cuub* available in Senegal comes from the Gambia, Guinea, or Guinea Bissau. Its dye is often a deep hue of indigo, and it ranges to green, brown, and purple. *Cuub* made with synthetic dyes come in a much wider range of colors, including gold, saffron, and red.

The confectioning of clothes is a craft industry in Senegal. It employs numerous spinsters, weavers, dyers, tailors, and embroiderers, mostly men, in small workshops on street corners in every town. While the unadorned workaday *legoos* dress can be sewn together by virtually any woman, with or without access to a sewing machine, both men and women have their *boubous* tailored by professionals. Not only are these outfits hand tailored, they are also high-maintenance. It is not enough that they simply be clean. After they are laundered, they must be starched and then beaten with wooden mallets for hours in order to create a stiff sheen. If they pale a bit after such treatment, they are redyed.

All but the very poorest people have two wardrobes: a traditional wardrobe of *pagnes, boubous,* and caftans, and a Western wardrobe. The traditional cloths are always worn on Muslim religious holidays and for family events, but otherwise, in their everyday lives, people oscillate freely between traditional and Western clothing. Young people are especially fond of Western attire. The rapper look—oversized pants, sports jersey, tennis shoes, and a baseball cap—has become ubiquitous among urban youth. Counterfeit versions of such labels as Nike, Levis, Chanel, and Gucci are displayed prominently. Still, despite the allure of global fashion and the lifestyle it promises, the Senegalese are committed to pursuing their own brand of *élégance,* based on local craftsmanship, fabrics, and traditions. And while container loads of used clothes and factory seconds shipped from the developed countries of the north continue to make clothing affordable for almost everyone, those with means continue to spend a considerable part of their incomes on high-quality traditional dress and patronize the craftsmen who can produce it.

HAIR AND JEWELRY

Second only to her wardrobe in importance is a woman's hairstyle. As with fabric designs, hairstyles are always changing, and they provide great leeway for personal expression. A woman's hair is always "done" in one way or another. Little girls have their hair tightly braided in cornrows by their older sisters to keep it out of the way. By puberty, girls are trying out a wide range of styles, but it is the young women who spend the most time and effort on their hair. Groups of young women organize daylong hair-braiding sessions in their homes, where they style one another's hair according to the latest fashion magazines. Artificial hair extensions are commercially available. Braided into their own hair, these extensions permit women to create ever more spectacular hairdos. Bleaching, streaking, and straightening are also common. Most mature women keep their hair in a headscarf or turban when they are in public. Yet they too have their hair carefully done up, preferably by a professional hairdresser. Hair is almost as big a business as clothing is. Women have their hair done for every special occasion, be it a religious celebration, national holiday, or family event. Hairdressing products account for a good deal of the cosmetics market, which includes a very controversial assortment of skin-lightening creams and lotions. There are major national and international hairdressing competitions and awards shows on TV.

And then there is jewelry. Gold is the precious metal preferred by women, who wear an assortment of gold necklaces, bracelets, earrings, rings, hairpins, and broaches. There was a time when a woman's wealth *was* her jewelry, and

that is still partly the case today. Beyond quantifiable economic consider-
ations, jewelry is still an indicator of a woman's social status and the ability
of her husband to provide her with gifts. Men's jewelry consists mostly of
silver rings and bracelets, some of which contain *téere,* or special encapsulated
talismans.

6

Family and Gender

SENEGALESE SOCIETY CAN be categorized as traditional. Both African and Islamic traditions shape family life, gender relations, and the socialization of children. As in all traditional societies, the family is central to an individual's sense of self and place. The family is not just a social unit, defining the position and status of its members in the community. It is also an economic unit. Solidarity and sharing of resources within the family, determined by gender, age, and filiation (paternal and maternal), are the only forms of material security many people ever enjoy.

The Wolof term *kër* means both "house" and "family." One carries one's *kër* with one wherever one goes. Identification with home and family thus runs deep. Whatever an individual might do, especially in public, he or she will refrain from dishonoring the family. While the obligation to honor one's parents and family is incumbent on all, it weighs especially heavily on women. The behavior of wives, daughters, and sisters is seen as a barometer of the order reigning in the household. Women are always expected to act with *sañse* (honor) and *sutra* (discretion) and are severely sanctioned by their husbands and fathers if they appear to have acted otherwise.

Matrilineality, which refers to maternal filiation, is as important as paternal filiation in determining the identity, status, and social position of offspring. Many Senegalese men carry their mother's name as well as their patronym, but this was far more common in the past. Until the late nineteenth century, when Islamic family law began to replace traditional law, a woman's property was inherited by her brother's sons rather than by her own.

Authority and power were also inherited through the mother. From a patrilineal perspective, Kayor, for example, was ruled by a single dynasty, the Fall, from the time of its independence from Jolof in 1549 to its conquest by the French in 1886. Yet, six noble *garmi* lineages—the Mouyôy, Wagadou, Sogno, Guelwaar, Dorobé, and Guedj—competed for power within the dynastic system. Simply being the legitimate son of a king was not sufficient for a royal prince to lay claim to the throne. He also had to be *garmi* on his mother's side. It was his *garmi* matrilineage that would support him against his paternal brothers and cousins from other matrilineages. And if he came to power as king, he was likely to choose his closest confidants and councillors from within his own matrilineage, and to take his first wife from among his mother's relatives.

Perhaps nowhere more than in the Sufi orders is Senegal's tradition of matrilineal transmission of power more evident today. As with the royal families of the precolonial era, each of today's Sufi lineages has a number of maternal families attached to it. The Mbacké sheikhs, for example, choose wives principally from the Bousso, Diakhaté, and Lô families; the Sy sheikhs of Tivaounane are divided between the Ndiaye and the Niang. The caliphs of the orders always choose their councillors from among their maternal relatives, and their sons tend to take a first wife from their mother's family.

FAMILY LIFE

Senegalese families are both large and extended. The average Senegalese household has between 9 and 10 members, while, on average, every Senegalese woman will have four or five children in her lifetime. The extended nature of Senegalese families is twofold. On the one hand, polygamy is widely practiced; about one-third of men have two or more wives. And on the other, grandparents and members of lateral lineages, such as uncles, aunts, nieces, nephews, and cousins, frequently live together in a family compound.

Polygamy is a common African marital practice, and it is sanctioned in Islam. Islamic law allows a man to be married to up to four women at the same time. While Senegal is a secular state, its family code permits this Islamic practice. Polygamy is always incremental. A young man will marry and start a family. Only after a decade or more will he have the financial and material means to take a second wife. In effect, taking an additional wife means, at the very least, building an additional house in the compound. It also means paying the dowry—in Senegal, as in much of Black Africa, it is the groom who pays the dowry to the bride's family. For men, the taking of additional wives is not simply a matter of sexual fulfillment. It is a marker of elevated social status or wealth. The biggest constraint to multiplying the number of wives, apart from money, is space. Polygamous households are far more problematic in urban housing environments, where living space is finite and expensive, than in rural ones, where compounds can be extended relatively easily. In fact, rural households are almost twice as likely to be polygamous than urban ones. In the city, marrying a second or third wife may mean having to buy an additional villa or apartment, something only the very rich can afford.

There are also historical reasons why polygamy is prevalent in agricultural settings. Until the middle of the twentieth century, the main constraining factor to increased agricultural production was labor, land being relatively abundant and accessible. Rural households thus resorted to several techniques to increase the labor pool. Domestic and agricultural slavery was one way of doing this. Another was to take many wives and produce many children, as both of these labor categories participated in production. Powerful nobles and wealthy warriors were known to have had dozens of wives and countless numbers of children. Even Muslim clerics and Sufi sheikhs resorted to this technique, as it had political benefits as well; a marriage was a secure way of sealing a strategic alliance.

Today, Senegalese law determines the manner in which polygamy is practiced. A groom must declare in the first marriage contract whether he intends to take more than one wife. This is supposed to protect the bride from an unhappy surprise later in her marriage. In practice, though, this clause of the marriage contract can be breached with relative impunity. Taken to court, the husband may be penalized with a fine. While the first wife could file for divorce for breach of contract, in reality she can only do this if she has the means to provide for herself and her children.

Senegal has one of the highest rates of polygamous marriages in the world, and the practice is currently a highly contested social issue. It is regularly debated in the press and in broadcast media, and it is a recurrent theme in plays, novels, and movies. Much of this debate is among women. For every woman who expresses a critical opinion of the practice, there seems to be another who extols its benefits: shared workload in the house, shared child rearing, and freedom from the daily obligation of serving the husband. Nonetheless, Senegal's feminist groups and women's associations are unanimous in calling for this patriarchic practice to be abolished or abandoned.

Beyond daily household activities and challenges, family life is punctuated by life-cycle events. All families begin with a marriage, and marriage is preceded by courtship. Some marriages are arranged by the parents without the involvement of the bride and groom, but this is increasingly rare. In some cases, a Sufi sheikh can arrange a marriage between the offspring of two of his followers, or he might be approached for help by a young man having difficulty finding a bride. For most young people, finding a marriage partner is a challenge. A man must be financially secure, preferably with a regular source of income, if he hopes to gain the consent of a woman's parents. During courtship he must prove his worth by providing impressive gifts to the woman's family. These might include household appliances (such as a sewing machine), livestock (in rural areas), and expensive bolts of cloth. Furthermore, there is the issue of the dowry. It is the groom who must provide the dowry, which could amount to a year's salary. And then there is the cost of the wedding itself, which is also paid for by the groom and his family. Because of all these monetary factors, and given Senegal's dire economic circumstances, marriages are increasingly being delayed; many men in their thirties are still bachelors, and many young women prefer a polygamous marriage to an established older man than the long wait for a younger man to muster the necessary resources. Dire economic conditions also help explain why child marriages, arranged between parents when their children are still infants, are becoming rarer.

The marriage itself is both religious and social. The religious part of the ceremony is rather brief; the male representatives of the bride's and groom's families finalize the arrangement with the imam of the local mosque or with their sheikh. Neither the groom nor the bride is present. Once the entirety of the dowry has been delivered to the bride's family, the date of the marriage is set. The celebrations, which involve music and dance, refreshments, and the reception of numerous guests, start separately at the houses of the bride and the groom. Each household butchers a cow or some sheep to feed the assembly. *Bisaab, jinjéer,* grilled meats, sweets, soft drinks, and tea are served. Because most houses are too small, much of the celebration occurs on the street outside, where rented awnings and chairs are set up. Needless to say, the entire neighborhood participates in the happy occasion. The partying starts in the afternoon and goes all night. In the early hours of the morning, the bride travels to the groom's house. From there they go together to their own house, leaving the guests to continue the party. Feasting and socializing go on for several days. The honeymoon lasts a week, but it is hardly an intimate affair, as well-wishing friends, relatives, and neighbors crowd the newlyweds' house.

Naming ceremonies, called *ngénte* in Wolof but commonly referred to as "baptisms," or *baptême* in French, are smaller one-day affairs. The naming of a newborn occurs on the seventh or eighth day following birth. The first week of life is considered extremely dangerous for a baby. The baby and the mother remain secluded in the house, as the mother had done during most of the pregnancy, and only the closest family members may visit. Great precaution is taken to protect the child from both visible and hidden threats. Only when the baby has survived the first week is it "born" socially. The ceremony occurs in the parents' home. The infant's head is shaved, and the sheikh or imam is called in to whisper the baby's name in his or her ear, along with appropriate religious incantations and prayers. The day's festivities can then begin. Griots turn up to extol the child's lineage. Family members and neighbors come bearing gifts. A sheep or a goat is slaughtered and a large midday meal prepared. In the afternoon there is music and dancing for the guests. Refreshments are served as the party extends well into the night.

The next life-cycle event, chronologically, is circumcision. Like polygamy, circumcision is a deeply established African practice that has been reinforced by Islamic precepts. All of Senegal's ethnic groups had traditional initiation practices involving circumcision, but these have been progressively replaced by the simpler Islamic practice. Traditional initiation, which marks the passage from childhood to manhood, used to take place after puberty, when boys were about 15 or even older, and it was always collective. The group of boys was isolated from other members of society, usually in a special grove containing some of the community's protective spirits. Physical circumcision was only one event in a process that could last for weeks or even months. While healing from the physical trauma of the operation, the boys would learn secret knowledge related to life forces that would permit them to be successful farmers, hunters, and warriors. These secrets were conveyed in secret songs. At the close of the process, the young men returned to the community and were received with feasting and dancing. Men who experienced initiation in this way became socially bonded as a single cohort, or *mbootaay*.

This type of comprehensive initiation is becoming rarer with each generation. It is currently practiced only among the Sereer, the Mandinka, and other small groups in the south and east. In Sedhiou, Kolda, and Mbour, Kankurang holidays, which celebrate the return of circumcised youth to the community, are major public festivals involving music and dance.

While not absolutely obligatory, circumcision of male children is highly recommended in Islam and is standard practice. Some Senegalese baby boys are clinically circumcised shortly after birth, but most undergo the operation later, when they are between 5 and 8 years old. Nowhere near as elaborate as the former traditional ceremonies, such circumcision is still done collectively. After a period of psychic, moral, and religious preparation, the eligible boys of a lineage, village, or neighborhood, dressed in white frocks and caps, spend several days together in the care of an elder, usually a member of the blacksmith caste. The boys must display courage and self-control the entire time. Their release following recovery is celebrated in their homes and in the streets, with dance parties called *kasag*.

Girls, too, have traditionally undergone a form of circumcision-initiation, called excision. Excision, or female genital cutting, involves the removal of part of the external genitals and is practiced right across the Sahelo-Sudanic zone, from Senegal to Yemen. Less ceremonious than the circumcision of boys, excision is practiced in the girl's house by a woman specialist. The practice is extremely painful, sometimes deadly, and is known to impact the health of women for the rest of their lives. Nationally, it is estimated that about one-quarter of Senegalese women submitted to the operation as girls, but the proportion is much higher in regions such as the Futa Toro, the upper Casamance, Fuladou, and the South East, and among ethnic groups such as the Halpulaaren and the Mandinka. The practice is far less common in urban areas. Since the mid-1990s, governmental agencies, national NGOs, and Islamic institutions have actively combated the practice of excision. Islamic scholars and Sufi sheikhs are keen to emphasize that excision has no foundation in the Koran or Islamic tradition. Nonetheless, it is women who are ultimately responsible for its continued practice. Women are the ones who perform the operation, and they only do so at the express invitation of the girl's mother. The last decade has seen very public declarations by traditional cutters who have foresworn the practice and committed themselves to educating mothers about its ill effects.

Death and burial are treated according to recommended Islamic or Christian practice. A Muslim funeral is usually held on the day the death occurs, or at the very latest on the morrow. Upon learning of a death, family members, friends, and neighbors immediately congregate at the house of the bereaved family. Men and women assemble in separate parts of the house, and the crowd eventually spills out into the street. Community leaders and heads of households take turns eulogizing the departed, relating edifying anecdotes, and reminiscing. Meanwhile, the body of the departed is washed by a senior family member, often the eldest son or daughter. The body is then wrapped in a simple shroud to be taken to the cemetery. Only the men folk accompany the body, on foot, to the cemetery. Graves are simple affairs. A small gravestone marks the head. If the family can afford to have it engraved, it will carry the name, birth and death dates, and perhaps a short religious phrase. Senegalese Catholics bury their dead according to the rites of the church. The body of the deceased is laid in a coffin. The funeral service is held in a church and the body laid to rest in a Christian cemetery.

GENDER AND THE ROLE OF WOMEN

The role of women in contemporary Senegal reflects the complex interface of African, Islamic, and modern Western traditions. As in the rest of sub-Saharan Africa, women have always had a strong presence in the public sphere, in society, and in the economy. On the other hand, Islamic law promotes a patriarchic family and tends to relegate women to the private sphere. Both of these traditions continue to affect women today.

The elevated position of women in precolonial times is best exemplified by their political roles. The chief woman at court held the title of *lingeer,* or queen mother. The *lingeer* was usually either the mother or a maternal sister of the reigning king. She exercised real power, especially over crown property, as she was its custodian. The *lingeers* of Kayor, for example, had rights to all the revenue produced by the lucrative salt pans of Gandiol. *Lingeers* were also important during interregnums and succession disputes. They always strove to have another royal prince from their own lineage enthroned, thus perpetuating the power of their *garmi* family within the dynasty and the state. Occasionally, they held very real political power as well. This was the case of Njemböt and Ndata Yala. In succession, these two sister *lingeers* virtually ruled the kingdom of Walo from 1830 until 1855—the nominal kings, their sons and husbands, being but proxies under their control. Senegal's most famous *lingeer* was Yassine Boubou of Kayor. Her political exploits during the Tubenan War (1673–1677) are legendary and continue to inspire contemporary writers and artists. At another level, the *lingeer* is also a model of matronly values. Thus, it can be said that there is a *lingeer* in every great house today.

The Métis *signares* offer another model of powerful, independent women in Senegalese history. *Signares* were the offspring of African women and European merchants (Portuguese, Dutch, French, more rarely English). The European wives of these merchants were discouraged from following them to Africa because of the health risks. Consequently, the merchants contracted "country marriages" with African women. Sometimes the African wives were slaves, but others were of noble birth. The fact that merchants selected wives from aristocratic lineages was related to their desire to promote their businesses up-country. European men rarely lived more than a few years along the African coast because they were susceptible to its various fevers. In fact, African wives were crucial to maintaining the health of their European husbands until they died or went home. When this happened, the wives and their *métis* offspring inherited the business and the properties, as well as the merchant's patronym. Moreover, girls born from these unions, fluent and sometimes even literate in European languages, often ended up marrying the next generation of merchants arriving from Europe.

Signares are remembered mostly for their exquisite taste and their patronage of musicians and artists. The menus of the sumptuous meals they prepared for guests, accompanied by fine local palm wines and imported spirits from

France, were recorded in contemporary documents. Their elegant fashions and headdresses have already been alluded to in the previous chapter. Yet, the *signares* were successful businesswomen as well. They owned houses, ships, and slaves, and they employed men. By the middle of the eighteenth century, fully three-quarters of the registered properties in Gorée belonged to Métis women. Names and activities of many *signares* are known to us through the archives. Bibiana Vaz of Cacheu (modern Guinea Bissau) owned a two-masted ship, among other vessels, and managed an extensive trading network. Similarly, La Belinguère was the indispensable intermediary for all Europeans trading along the Gambia River in the 1680s. She spoke Portuguese, French, and English, and her hospitality, fashion, and cuisine were legendary. Senhora Catarina of Rufisque acted as a commercial agent for the king of Kayor in the 1660s. She served as an interpreter during negotiations, and her slaves traded up-country in her behalf. She was a practicing Catholic but patronized Muslim clerics as well. Her neighbor, Signora Philippa, turned her house in Rufisque into a Catholic chapel. Louise de Saint-Jean, daughter of a *signare* of Gorée, founded the Congregation of the Sisters of the Sacred Heart of Mary in 1858. This was the first Catholic order to be created *in* Africa. Thus, the *signares* are not just fashion icons from the past; they are models of the woman entrepreneur. Their achievements, and those of Senegalese women more generally, are remembered and displayed in the Henriette Bathily Museum of Women in Gorée.

Beyond the prestigious examples of the *lingeers* and the *signares,* Senegalese women have always been important social and cultural actors. They are especially present in commerce. As in much of sub-Saharan Africa, the local marketplace is women's space. Most of the merchants are women, as are most of the clients, and this is as true of the marketing of fresh farm produce (fruits and vegetables) and fish as it is of the socially crucial and financially lucrative cloth trade. Of all proximity commerce, only the livestock market is male dominated.

Women are active in virtually every economic sector and profession today. There are women doctors, lawyers, journalists, teachers, and professors. Perhaps more important, women run a good part of the "real" economy, that is, the informal sector of petty trades and street commerce, and they are more likely to organize themselves into business associations than are their male counterparts. They are responsible, for example, for most *tontines. Tontines* are rotating savings and credit associations where members contribute savings to a fund and then take turns borrowing and reimbursing sums. Women are also the main beneficiaries of microfinance institutions which lend small sums at low or no interest. Women benefit from these informal-sector credit institutions, which they administer, in order to invest in personal or family businesses. Women have always controlled the revenue they produce within a household. This is especially important to understanding conjugal dynamics in polygamous families, where the husband and several wives each contribute revenue.

Women are active in religion as well, always an important part of Senegalese society and culture. They are central to traditional religious rites and practices. Priestesses tend to most of Senegal's surviving *tuur* shrines, and women still practice exorcism ceremonies, such as the *ndëp* of the Lebu. Women are also spiritually active in the Islamic context. They run their own *dahiras,* or recitation circles, within Senegal's Sufi orders, and some Senegalese Sufi women have attained the high rank of *sheikhah,* which is extremely rare elsewhere in the Muslim world. Soxna Mariama Niass of the Kaolack Tijaniyya (b. 1932) is a reputed Islamic scholar who specializes in women's issues, and Adja Khar Mané and Oumy Souko are *sheikhahs* of the Qadiriyya. Soxna Maïmouna Mbacké (1926–2000), Sheikh Ahmadou Bamba's youngest daughter, had a large following of disciples, both men and women. Since the 1950s, the tomb of Ahmadou Bamba's saintly mother, Mame Diarra Bousso (1833–1866), in Porokhane, has become an important pilgrimage center for Mourides and for Mouride women especially. Considered a paragon of piety and submission to her husband, Mame Diarra is also believed to help those in need who express a wish at her tomb.

Senegal's most well-known female Sufi was Soxna Magat Diop (1917–2004), also a Mouride. Daughter of Baye Fall sheikh Abdoulaye Iyakhine Niakhité (1886–1943), she inherited leadership of her father's disciples when he died. Like Soxna Maïmouna Mbacké, Soxna Magat Diop taught the Koran to both male and female students. When she died, leadership of this branch of the Baye Fall Mourides was contested between her eldest surviving sister, Soxna Seybata Aîdara, and her eldest daughter, Soxna Bintou Massamba Mbacké (b. 1934). Soxna Bintou Massamba heads a national NGO that targets indigent and orphaned children.

Finally, it is in the field of popular culture, singing and dance especially, that women are most active today. At street level, it is the women who initiate the *tànn-béer,* or improvised street party involving *sabar* drumming and dancing. Women maintain a distinctive form of poetry called *taasu,* which consists of often acerbic, witty lines used to comment on each other's intimate lives. Women were always important to the oral griot tradition, but with the arrival of radio, records, and TV, they have been far more successful than their male counterparts in reaching a mass audience, combining traditional praise singing with pop acoustics and lyrics. Since independence, nearly all the most successful female vocalists have come from griot families, and all the successful griot pop stars have been women.

Yet despite these high-profile public roles in the economy, in religion, in show business, and in community life, women are still valued mostly for their roles as wives and mothers. Both African and Islamic traditions reinforce this conservative attitude toward what a woman's place should be, and this attitude helps explain why women have had so little space in national politics. There have been women politicians since independence, but they have been comparatively few in number and have rarely held top positions.

The first political career woman, in the modern sense, was Caroline Faye Diop, wife of the independence-era politician Demba Diop. In 1963 she became the first woman elected to the National Assembly. Both she and her husband were members of Senghor's UPS party, and Demba Diop, until his assassination in 1967, was one of Senghor's top ministers. Following his death, Caroline Faye Diop held a string of ministerial posts during the 1970s and 1980s, the first woman to do so. Since then, however, few women politicians have been as successful. There has always been a handful of women parliamentarians, and at least one or two women in the cabinet at any given time, but these cabinet positions have been traditional "women's posts": health, education, youth, family, social affairs, culture, and so forth.

The 2000–2001 presidential and legislative elections marked a watershed in women's representation. In 2000 Marième Wane Ly, secretary general of the Parti pour la Renaissance Africaine (PARENA), became the first woman to run for the presidency. The elections brought Abdoulaye Wade to office and launched the political career of Mame Madior Boye (b. 1940). Like Wade, Boye is a lawyer and was already a magistrate when he appointed her minister of justice and keeper of the seals in his first cabinet. She was the first woman to hold the post. In March 2001 Wade appointed her prime minister, making her the first woman to hold that post as well. In November 2002 President Wade dismissed his entire cabinet, including his prime minister, in the wake of the capsizing of the Joola ferryboat, an unprecedented national disaster. She was, however, back in the new cabinet, this time as minister of defense—another first for a woman. Since then, Mame Madior Boye has had an international diplomatic career, serving with the African Union on issues related to the protection of civilians in conflict and democratic transition, most notably in the Democratic Republic of Congo.

Children and Youth

Senegal has a very young population: 57 percent is under 20 years old, and 42 percent is under 15. These children and young people have a culture all their own. Typical of societies elsewhere in Black Africa, this culture is distinguished by age cohort associations, or *mbootaay*. Children of similar age not only play and study together, but they also become socially active together, as a group. This is largely the legacy of traditional rural society, where both boys and girls are given specific agricultural and household tasks. The most spectacular manifestations of age cohort social structures are the traditional initiation ceremonies discussed earlier. While these ceremonies are increasingly rare, the associative nature of growing up is still very strong. And it has found a new dynamic in urban settings.

Given how large extended polygamous families can be, with numerous sisters and brothers of various ages and parentage living in the same house, children are more or less left to look after one another. Older girls in particular are responsible for younger siblings. More generally, parents like to let a young child fend for himself or herself in the house to see how the personality develops before attempting any type of education. In such a highly competitive environment, the child must quickly learn appropriate social skills. As with children everywhere, much of this learning takes the form of play. In most households, where resources barely cover basic needs, children make their own games and toys. Classic favorites include rag dolls, hopscotch, skipping, hide-and-seek, and hoops.

Outside the home, boys and girls live separate social lives. Girls are given so many household chores—helping with cleaning, looking after siblings, running errands, and so forth—that they have little external social life. Most of their socializing is done inside the house with other family members, visiting relatives, and the girls next door. Boys, on the other hand, are encouraged to play outside from an early age. They first acquire social skills with other boys of similar age who live on their street.

In some ways, the creation of *mbootaay* age cohort associations is a natural outcome of this neighborhood-level socialization. Age cohort associations include all the children of a certain age in a given street or neighborhood. These associations undertake a number of activities throughout the year. Typical activities include organizing informal football matches between neighborhoods or planning street parties. Neighborhood street dance parties, called *furrëls,* are organized on national civic holidays and other special occasions. They require a fair amount of preparation: rental of tents, chairs, and a sound system; preparation of refreshments; service activities during the party; and cleanup afterward. A cover charge at the door helps pay the expenses incurred. Various tasks are apportioned to age cohort associations, both male and female, according to their capacity to contribute. Though adults attend the party, they hardly participate in its organization. Associations of older children mentor those of younger ones through these activities, and they all take great pride in their respective contributions. The Set Setal movement of 1990, described in chapter 4, was only possible because youth were already organized and mobilized at street level and had experience managing their own activities in this way.

Children's education begins in preschool, with the *daara,* which is a Koranic school. Children begin attending at the age of four or five. The instruction involves memorizing chapters of the Koran. In the process, children learn the Arabic alphabet. More boys than girls attend the *daaras,* and the girls are usually seated in a separate class or behind the boys. Most *daaras* are affiliated with one Sufi order or another and are under the care of a particular sheikh, who teaches from his house. Parents choose which *daara* to send their child to. Some *daaras* are free, but many require payment of some kind (monetary or in kind). *Daaras* have acquired a bad reputation, as many unscrupulous sheikhs send the boys out to beg in the street or door-to-door before they begin their lessons each day. This practice is increasingly being seen as abusive, and Cheikh Hamidou Kane, well-known author of *Ambiguous Adventure,* has recently championed the cause of these young begging pupils.

The *daara* is the only formal education many children ever receive. Primary school attendance varies from 60 to 70 percent, depending on the region and rural/urban and gender dichotomies; more boys attend school than girls, and attendance rates increase in cities. When children are not attending school, it is usually because they are required to work at home or in the family's business. Girls must care for babies and infants while their mothers work outside the house, while boys must help their fathers in the fields, with livestock, or in some petty trade. By the time they reach high school age, attendance rates fall to about 20 percent. Most parents simply cannot afford to send numerous children to school. Though public schooling is free, pupils still need school supplies, textbooks, transportation, and decent clothing (shoes, shirts, dresses, etc.)—all of which cost money. Moreover, given the extremely high unemployment rate among young people, including those with high school completion certificates, matriculations, and university degrees, there is little faith among parents that this expense constitutes any kind of investment in the future.

Youth and their parents are increasingly turning to informal and vocational-type strategies. Boys thus become apprentices in workshops or garages, while their sisters learn dressmaking or hairdressing in an existing salon. This form of education is seen as better preparation for the real world. Furthermore, the disjunction between the *daara* and the public schools on the one hand, and real life on the other, is keenly felt by children. *Daaras* teach in Arabic, while public schools teach in French. Neither of these is the mother tongue or the first language of the children who attend, and neither is particularly useful in the "real" economy of petty trades, crafts, and services, let alone farm work.

Young people remain socially and economically dependent on their parents until they marry. In the absence of employment opportunities, this crucial moment can be postponed indefinitely. Delayed marriage can cause tension in family life. Unmarried adult men and women who continue to live under their father's roof must submit to his authority. Only those who can secure regular income can gain any kind of independence.

Youth culture is very much a street culture, and it is increasingly global in its referents. Music, dance, and fashion play important roles in youth identity. And while Senegalese traditions in these areas are lively, international Western styles are always present. This has to do partly with access to global media (satellite TV, Internet chat rooms, etc.) and partly with the ubiquity of global commercial brands and consumerism. There is also a growing number of Senegalese living abroad, in Western Europe and in North America. These *modou-modou*, as they are called, return to Senegal regularly, flashing the latest gadgets. They have become icons for the young. Like youth everywhere, Senegalese youth aspire to "the good life" they know is out there. Yet daily they must face the reality that their families and communities are too poor to afford it. Young people thus dream of the chance to go abroad, to Italy or to Canada, where they too can make it big. It is seen as the only way out of poverty and hopelessness. In the last few years illegal migration has reached a crisis point. Young men and women crowd onto tiny fishing boats in an attempt to reach European territory through the Canary Islands. Many boats never make it, and the death toll at sea cannot even be known.

Meanwhile, a new icon of youth success has emerged, the call-center employee. Call centers have proliferated in Dakar as French corporations outsource customer services. They employ mostly young, educated youth—men and women in equal measure—of which Dakar has an abundant supply. Call-center employees speak flawless French with a neutral accent and answer to names like "Sonia" and "Patrick." There are an estimated 5,000 such white-collar jobs in Dakar. These young workers still live at home, but now they contribute to the household budget and they have disposable income to spend on the dream lifestyle and positional consumer products like cell phones and MP3 players.

In its own way, the diffusion of cell phones over the past decade has had a revolutionary impact on youth culture. In the days before cell phones, telephone use in families wealthy enough to afford a land line was closely monitored by the male head of household, the phone being kept under lock and key. Cell phones in the purses of women and in the jeans pockets of young people means that husbands and fathers can no longer hope to control the lives of wives and teenage children the way they used to. Dating techniques have been refined by the cell phone, and literate young people are connecting online as well.

7

Social Customs and Lifestyle

SENEGALESE SOCIETY IS thoroughly civil and deeply democratic. Its social customs are firmly rooted in an ancient rural civilization where family honor, pride in lineage, and generosity and hospitality toward strangers are sacrosanct. Its modern democratic practices and institutions are grounded in a long experience with global exchange and urban life. Furthermore, the sense of social peace and optimism that permeates everyday life, despite decades of economic woes, is based on an open understanding of public life, one that synthesizes the universal values of African, Islamic, and Western civilizations and that embraces modernity in surprising ways.

Senegal is the land of *teraanga,* or hospitality. *Teraanga* is a key concept at the heart of interpersonal relations. It connotes civility, honor, and consideration for others, whoever they may be. Practicing *teraanga* in daily life requires an attitude of respect, openness, and tolerance. It also means that people take the time to deal with others as humans. People regularly inquire about each other's families, about the health and well-being of loved ones, and about their activities and affairs. No simple human interaction, like purchasing an item at the corner store, is too insignificant to warrant this caring disposition.

SOCIAL STRUCTURES, CASTE, AND THE LEGACY OF SLAVERY

Senegal's social structure today is still marked by deeply embedded distinctions of caste and slave ancestry. The caste system has characterized most

Sahelo-Sudanic societies historically, including all of Senegal's main ethnic groups: the Wolof, Sereer, Lebu, Toucouleur, Peul, Diola, and Mandinka. At the heart of this system is a subdivision of society according to notions of purity with regard to both the spiritual and material worlds. Simply put, certain categories of people have access to certain types of spirits, and this gives them control over specific physical elements. Moreover, these qualities are inherited from one's parents and are fixed at birth, which makes social mobility all but impossible, at least theoretically.

Wolof society was built on the primary distinction among "free" people (*géér*), artisans (*ñeeño*), and slaves (*jaam*). The *géér* were "free" of any attachment to a particular trade. They were direct producers of food; thus this group included farmers, herders, and fishermen. They alone had access to land, and they alone could deal with the powerful spirits that controlled agricultural production and animal husbandry. The *ñeeño,* on the other hand, were "true" castes, as they were attached by birth to a specific trade or craft. Unable to farm land, they earned their livelihoods by transforming mineral, vegetable, or animal matter. They alone could relate to the powerful spirits that resided in, and controlled, these materials. This binary social division between free and caste predates the beginning of history and was most likely set in place during the agricultural revolution of the Neolithic era. The categories were fixed and endogamous, meaning that one was born into a particular caste, a status inherited from the father, and could not marry outside the group. The binary system was soon complicated by a third category, the *jaam* (slaves). *Jaam* were, by definition, not free. Enslaved following defeat in battle, or for perpetrating a crime or major social transgression, these individuals lost whatever status they formerly had. They no longer had access to the spirit world, and their labor belonged to their *géér* masters.

With the growth of monarchic state structures, beginning over a thousand years ago, the caste system was further complicated by finer distinctions of economic function. The *géér* were differentiated between those who controlled land and could tax agricultural produce, the *jàmbur* (landlords), and those who were simple peasants, the *baadoolo.* The *jàmbur* constituted the class of nobles or aristocrats. They were further distinguished between local chiefs (the *laman*), those who could exercise political power (the *buur*), and the *garmi* matrilineages. Each social "order" had a specific political role related to its control of land and human resources. As the practice of Islam grew, an additional *jàmbur* group appeared, the *sëriñ,* or Muslim cleric. Like other *jàmbur,* the *sëriñ* controlled land and the labor of peasants and slaves, they could exercise political authority, and they could employ various categories of artisans.

The *ñeeño,* or artisans, were likewise subdivided according to specialized trade. The *tëgg* were blacksmiths. They worked metal, iron mostly, for making agricultural tools and household utensils. They also worked precious metals like gold and thus were jewelers as well as smiths. They had special access to the awesome spiritual worlds of fire and earth and were thus feared for the secret sources of power they controlled. The *lawbe* were woodworkers, carpenters, and cabinet makers. They had privileged access to forest spirits and the spirits of trees. The *wuude* were leatherworkers. They produced not only shoes and household goods but also the harnesses and saddles needed for draft animals and cavalries. They worked with the hides of dead animals and thus were in close contact with some potentially malefic spirits. The *ràbb* were the weavers. They produced a range of cloth types for everyday use, elite use, and trade. As explained in chapter 3, the *géwél,* or griots, were specialists of orality. They were responsible for recording events and genealogies and for reciting them. They had power over the uttered word, which was considered a fearsome power indeed.

Among the slaves, too, a distinction arose between the *jaami-baadoolo,* a "personal" or "house" slave, and the *jaami-buur,* a "crown" slave in the service of the state. One group of crown slaves in particular, the *ceddo,* or "warriors," acquired great political power in the era of the transatlantic slave trade. They were the principal beneficiaries of the pillaging and slave raiding endemic at the time, and they had privileged access to high-value European exports like firearms, cloth, and alcohol. The *ceddo* were keenly aware of the spiritual dimensions of battle and combat. They took great pains to protect their bodies from every potential threat, and, ironically given their hostility toward Islamic practices, they patronized the Muslim clerics in order to obtain the most protective talismans.

The traditional elite in precolonial times were thus a landed aristocracy. The various categories of *jàmbur* owned or otherwise controlled agricultural villages worked by peasants, whom they taxed. They had a monopoly on political power, locally as well as in the monarchic system. These elite also patronized all the categories of tradesmen, as their economic productivity and lifestyles required various metal and wooden tools, jewelry, fine clothing, saddles and harnesses, and lots of praise singing. Theoretically, the political-economic social structure was extremely rigid. Individuals were born into their caste and could never leave it. Marriages between members of different castes, while not impossible, were rare. To marry below one's caste was dishonorable to one's family. The children of such marriages always assumed the status of the lower-caste parent. The reality of social relations, however, varied somewhat from this rigid theory. The *ceddo,* for example, were of slave status and thus, theoretically, were at the bottom of the social hierarchy. Yet by the eighteenth century they were among the most powerful groups, controlling strategic resources, exercising considerable power within the monarchies, and accumulating wealth, land, and slaves. In effect, some *ceddo* became far more powerful than many an ancient noble lineage of impeccable pedigree. Likewise, in the nineteenth century, certain clerical families, which had hitherto been peripheral to the system, married into the top aristocratic and noble lineages.

The complex social structures of the precolonial era have lost most of their political and economic validity today. Slavery was progressively abolished in the course of the second half of the nineteenth century. In rural areas the traditional land tenure systems of the past, with their social duties and prerogatives, were abolished soon after independence. In the formal economy of urban areas, jobs in manufacturing and the service sector are allocated according to skill, expertise, experience, training, and contacts, but not caste affiliation. Senegalese law recognizes no distinctions of caste, ethnicity, or religion (though gender disparity based on Islamic family law remains); all Senegalese are equal citizens. Moreover, Sufi orders have also actively combated traditional caste distinctions, stressing that they have no basis in Islam and that all Muslims are brothers. The Layène and the Niassène-Tjaniyya of Kaolack in particular have condemned caste distinctions as un-Islamic.

And yet, these distinctions remain deeply ingrained in social relations. Individuals are always acutely aware of their parents' origins and of their patrilineal and matrilineal backgrounds. If nothing else, patronyms are markers of such things. People with the last name Thiam were traditionally jewelers. The Laobé were woodworkers. The Ndiaye and the Diouf are of "free," if not always noble, ancestry. Even beyond these easy signifiers, people wear their origins on their sleeves, so to speak. Ancestry is a major concern in marriage, even today. Marriages between persons of *géér* and *ñeeño* ancestry are extremely rare, and when such marriages do occur, they are always cause for concern in the community. Slave ancestry, too, is taboo. Few will admit to it, yet its legacy persists, especially in rural areas. In villages, where the descendants of slaves and masters live in proximity to one another and continue to work the land, habitual social relations persist. The descendants of slaves still serve the families of their former masters and are still protected by them in various ways. People of griot descent still constitute a distinct social category. They see themselves as custodians and perpetrators of Senegal's oldest culture and customs. While people admire and respect them for their honed ability to express the spirit of things, they also fear them for their power to bring good or bad fortune to those they sing about.

And then there is the informal sector, or what is now increasingly being called the "real economy." The real economy comprises a host of petty trades mostly concentrated in urban and peri-urban areas. These activities include peddlers of fruit or household supplies; providers of services such as hairdressing, tailoring, embroidery, and laundry; manufacturing of utensils and toys from recycled material; the growing of garden vegetables; shoe repair; car washing; whole swathes of the construction industry (masons, joiners, plasterers, brick makers, welders); givers of private lessons; sidewalk snack bars; unlicensed taxis; and classic illegal activities such as prostitution, contraband, and drug dealing. The real economy, best observed at street level, is difficult to describe and even more difficult to measure accurately. The majority of people in urban areas earn their income in this sector.

As a sector, the real economy is far more dependent on underlying social structures than is the formal economy (civil service, manufacturing, salaried jobs). Extended family connections, lineage, home village, and relations with family members abroad are likely to determine the economic activity of an individual. These social structures, in turn, are those that have preserved traditional attitudes toward caste and slave origins.

COMMUNITIES: VILLAGE LIFE, THE NEIGHBORHOOD, AND STREET LIFE

In addition to social status and genealogical origin, individuals have a strong sense of community. This sense of community can be based on ethnic origin or Sufi affiliation. It can also have a more local basis and pertain to a single village or rural district, or to a particular neighborhood. It transcends the caste and lineage identities described earlier, which helps explain why social relations are far less volatile than they might otherwise be.

In many instances, community identity is built on Sufi affiliation. Village communities or urban neighborhoods may owe their very existence to the activities of a particular Sufi sheikh, who is considered a founding figure. The identity is perpetuated by descendants of the sheikh, who may, informally, wield substantial power within the community, as well as by the social and cultural activities of *dahiras*. Group recitations, called *njàng*, for example, are very popular local events. They are organized by a *dahira* in the courtyard of someone's house. A rented amplification system is set up, and invitations are sent out. Perhaps a well-known reciter of poetry will be invited to lead the group. The *njàng* starts in the evening and lasts until morning prayer. Women's *dahiras* may organize their own events, or else women will find a space next to the men. Given the amplification of the recitations, the whole neighborhood is invited to participate. Refreshments such as café touba and *bisaab* are served. Thursday night, the night before Friday prayer, is the preferred time for these important local religious and social events.

In some instances, sense of community is based on ethnic identity. Among the Sereer, the Toucouleur of the Futa Toro, and the Diola of the Casamance there are deeply felt communal ties that are expressed in a distinct language but also in music, dance, and cherished traditions such as wrestling. Since the 1960s the Futa Toro has been a region of out-migration. Generation after generation, one age cohort after another has left the Futa in search of jobs elsewhere. There are thus substantial Foutanké populations in Dakar and in the various regional capitals, as well as in Paris and cities abroad. This Foutanké diaspora remains very attached to its homeland. The Pulaar language, a proud Islamic heritage, and the Tijaniyya Sufi order are powerful factors of cultural unity that bind the sons and daughters of the Futa to that region. But the Foutanké of the diaspora are also attached to their particular township or province, called a *leydi,* which is a group of about a dozen closely related villages. In Dakar, as in France, migrants from Futa Toro have created associations on the basis of their home *leydi.* They raise funds for special projects, wells, and schools, and they maintain regular relations not only with the home township but with other associations from that township located elsewhere. The same is partially true of the Sereer, who have numerous home village–type associations in Dakar and other cities. Whether they are Christian or Muslim, the Sereer are proud of the traditional spiritual life experienced only in the home village. They value their home traditions and perpetuate pride in their local histories, wherever they happen to be living.

Urban community identities are also pronounced. The citizens of Saint Louis think very highly of their unique city. They are also very attached to their particular neighborhoods: the "South" and "North" quarters on the island itself, Ndar-Tout and Guet-Ndar on the ocean side, and Sor on the mainland. Likewise, in the greater Dakar metropolitan area there are Médina, Grand Dakar, Pikine, and Guediawaye identities, and similar neighborhood identities in regional cities such as Thiès, Diourbel, and Ziguinchor. These identities are produced and sustained through the multitude of informal *mbootaay* associations that seem to spring forth from every street. For the most part, these urban community identities are not so determined by ethnicity, religion, or Sufi affiliation. They are primarily based on the shared experience of living in proximity to one another. The *teraanga* of living together on the same street or in the same village creates the sense of community that is celebrated at each wedding, with each baptism, every time a *njàng* Sufi recitation rings out over loudspeakers, a local football match is played, a street party is organized, or a colorful mural is painted on a wall.

CELEBRATIONS

Senegal's community life and street culture are festive and celebratory. Local communities come together to celebrate life-cycle events like weddings and baptisms. They also celebrate Muslim and Christian holidays and national civic commemorations. Celebrations are always collective and, depending on the nature of the event, involve a variety of artistic forms, principally music, dance, and poetry. Fine clothing and individuals displaying the latest fashions and hairstyles are also a feature. Some events are celebrated everywhere at once, in all villages and neighborhoods, while others occur at a single place.

Most public holidays in Senegal are religious in nature, and all the principal Muslim and Christian holidays are observed. The main Sunni Muslim festivals are observed according to sanctioned Islamic practice. The Muslim year consists of 12 lunar months and is 11 days shorter than the solar Christian year. Muslim festivals therefore shift a bit each year in relation to the seasons and the civic calendar.

The most important Muslim holy day is Tabaski ('Îd al-Adhâ or 'Îd al-Kabîr in Arabic), held on the 10th of Dhû-l-Hijjah. Tabaski corresponds to the culmination of the *hajj* pilgrimage to the holy places in Mecca. It commemorates the prophet Abraham, who would have sacrificed his son Ismael at the command of God had God not produced a sacrificial a ram instead. As everywhere else in the Muslim world, every head of household must slaughter a ram on this occasion. Sheep are purchased in the days and weeks prior to the holiday and are fattened up for the event. For many poor families, the buying of a sheep constitutes a great expense, while wealthy families will sacrifice several rams. The day's commemoration begins with a collective midmorning prayer that all men attend. The prayer is held outdoors, on a designated prayer ground. When the men return home from prayer, they will sacrifice the sheep. The sheep are immediately skinned and butchered, and some grilled meat is consumed for lunch. The afternoon and evening are devoted to socializing with relatives, friends, and neighbors. Gifts and dishes of food are offered to poorer relatives, and children are given pocket money to buy candy. The consumption of mutton continues on the next day, and the day after that.

The second major Muslim holy day is Korite ('Îd al-Fitr in Arabic). Held on the first day of Shawwal, it marks the end of the holy month of Ramadân. Ramadân is the month of fasting and abnegation. Its observation is one of the five pillars of Muslim practice. During the entire month no food or drink may be consumed from the time the first light of day appears in the night sky to the time the sun sets. Sexual activity and smoking are also not permitted during the day. In fact, Muslims are to use the time to reflect on the hold that material and carnal desires have on the human spirit and to contemplate God. People refrain from being angry and irritable and attempt to make peace with those around them. They abandon frivolous entertainment and spend more time praying. Some people rise well before dawn to consume a light breakfast. Otherwise, no food or drink will be consumed for the remainder of the day.

The breaking of the fast occurs after sundown, when a light meal is served. A larger meal is served later in the evening. Only those who are able to fast conscientiously are expected to do so. Children, pregnant women and nursing mothers, and those who are ill or under duress are all exempt to various degrees. Non-Muslims, foreigners, and tourists are not bound to fast but are expected to maintain decorum by not eating, drinking, or smoking in public places during the day. Ramadân is an austere month and a time to be with family. Very little socializing occurs. People go about their daily tasks, slowly, and then return home for the night. Restaurants and bars are closed. No music or dance parties are organized.

The month ends with the Korite feast. When the new moon of Shawwal is spotted in the evening sky, the following day will be Korite. As with Tabaski, the day begins with a collective midmorning prayer at the prayer ground, to which men wear freshly laundered *grands boubous.* This is followed by a large family lunch, where many special dishes are served. The afternoon and evening are spent visiting relatives and neighbors. People ask for each other's forgiveness, so that any relations strained in the past year can get off to a fresh start. Candy and sweets are offered, and children are given coins. By nightfall, music and dancing have resumed, after the month-long abstention. Social visits continue over the next few days as well, until all obligations have been honored.

Tamxarit marks the Muslim new year. Technically, the Muslim year begins on the first day of Muharram, but its celebration in Senegal is held on the 10th day of that month (equivalent to 'Âshûrâ' in Arabic). Tamxarit is not really a religious holy day, but it is a very popular national civic holiday nonetheless. A traditional meal of Moroccan-style couscous, served with beef or chicken, is prepared. At nightfall, children dress up in adult clothes of the opposite sex—girls dress as men, and boys dress as women—and they take to the streets, going door to door asking for money and treats. This is the *taajabóon,* an old tradition of unknown origin and significance that has become attached to a date on the Muslim calendar. As with Halloween in America, not just children but young people have begun to celebrate *taajabóon* with dress-up parties.

The Mawlud celebration, the 12th of Rabî' al-Awwal, commemorates the birthday of the prophet Muhammad. The Mawlud is a very religious affair and is especially celebrated within the Sufi orders. Most of the commemoration consists of all-night vigils held in mosques and *zâwiyas.* Separate circles of male and female disciples recite poems in honor of Muhammad.

While all Sufi groups celebrate the Mawlud, it is particularly important to the Tijaniyya, who always hold a special recitation of Al-Busîrî's *Al-Burda* (a famous thirteenth-century ode to the Prophet) on the occasion. In Tivaouane this event is called the Gàmmu. Tivaouane's Gàmmu brings well over 1 million Tijani disciples to the city's *zâwiyas* and mosques.

Other important Sufi commemorations in Senegal include the Ngénte Gàmmu, the Laylat al-Qadr, and the Night of mid-Sha'bân. The Ngénte Gàmmu commemorates the naming of the prophet Muhammad a week after his birth (20th of Rabî' al-Awwal). Often called "baptism" in Senegal, the naming (*aqîqa* in Arabic) of the Prophet is especially celebrated by the Kounta-Qadiriyyah order, which holds a major pilgrimage in Ndiassane. The Laylat al-Qadr, or "Night of Power," occurs on a specially determined night during Ramadân. It marks the "sending down" of the Koran by God to humanity. It is celebrated by all-night poetry and Koranic recitations in mosques. The Night of mid-Sha'bân (14th–15th of Sha'bân) has many esoteric significations for Sufis. Like other holy nights, it is celebrated with much prayer and recitation. A major pilgrimage is held in the Mouride city of Darou Mousty on that occasion.

Senegal's largest Sufi celebration is Touba's Grand Màggal. It is held each year on the 18th of Safar to commemorate Sheikh Ahmadou Bamba Mbacké's exile to Gabon in 1895. It is actually a three-day event during which over a million Mouride pilgrims, along with high-ranking government officials and diplomats, congregate on the holy city. Pilgrims pray at Touba's Great Mosque, visit the tombs of the saint and other Sufi sheikhs, and make courtesy calls on the caliph general and other dignitaries. They also use the occasion to do some shopping, as Touba is one of the country's main commercial centers.

Apart from the Grand Màggal, Touba hosts a number of smaller *màggals* throughout the year. Each of the Mouride order's major lineages and subbranches holds its own celebration. Moreover, the secondary Mouride shrine towns—Darou Mousty, Mbacké Kayor, Darou Salam, and Porokhane—also organize annual *màggals,* and lesser Mouride pilgrimages are held in Saint Louis and Dakar as well. Some of these latter events are held according to the Christian calendar. Similarly, the 10-day spiritual retreat at Daaka, organized by the Tijaniyya of Madina Gounass, is held each year in April. It attracts between 600,000 and 700,000 pilgrims from across Senegal, neighboring countries, and overseas.

Christian holidays are also celebrated in Senegal. Christmas and Easter week are the main holy days for Catholics. They are celebrated in church, with masses, and are major family events. Feasts are prepared for these occasions, and they give rise to socializing and visits to relatives. Jesus, who is recognized as one of God's great prophets by Muslims generally, is held in particularly high esteem by the Layène Sufi order. Consequently, they hold a pilgrimage at their shrine in Cambérène on Christmas Day.

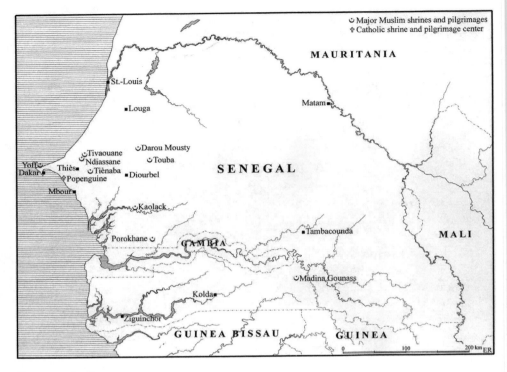

Shrines and pilgrimages.

The main Catholic pilgrimage in Senegal is held at Popenguine, home to a revered statue of the Black Madonna and Child. The statue is a copy of the one in Caen, France, and was brought to Popenguine in 1888. Popenguine is the object of an annual pilgrimage on the Pentecost. The pilgrims proceed on foot from Dakar to Popenguine, a distance of about 28 miles.

The Senegalese civic year is thus punctuated by mass religious commemorations, many of which are pilgrimages to specific holy places. These events are always widely covered by the national media. The major pilgrimages—Touba's Grand Màggal, Tivaouane's Gàmmu, and the Daaka of Madina Gounass— require months of preparation and close collaboration between the respective Sufi orders and government services (health services, transportation, policing). Civil servants are given leave to attend these events. The volume of traffic on these occasions severely taxes the country's clogged and potholed road network.

Senegal's most important civic holiday is Independence Day, April 4th. While there are some official aspects to the commemoration, such as the president's televised address to the nation, April 4th is a very popular celebration. Dance parties are organized locally, by neighborhood and street associations, though larger pop concerts may be held in stadiums. Local football matches and wrestling championships are also held.

Christmas and New Year's Eve are occasions for much partying as well. Dakar's bars and nightclubs are packed with dancers and revelers. Pop concerts are held in stadiums, as are professional wrestling matches. This holiday partying is not without its critics. Conservative and pious Muslim leaders regularly condemn these holidays as un-Islamic and manifestations of European/Western debauchery corrupting Senegalese youth. The consumption of alcohol and unsupervised promiscuity between the sexes are decried. Yet, despite these critiques, nightlife and partying are major features of urban life in Dakar, Saint Louis, Thiès, Mbour, Kaolack, and Ziguinchor. Dancing is an important form of expression, especially for women. Their long tradition of dancing underlies modern, contemporary manifestations in dance clubs.

Electioneering constitutes another type of civic event. Elections have been held regularly since the 1880s. They became mass affairs in the 1950s, when voting rights were extended to all adult men and women across the country. In order to get elected, all political parties try to mobilize as much grassroots support as possible. Some mobilization and outreach are done through the mass media, but most must still be done on the ground, at street level in communities, neighborhoods, and villages. Electoral campaigns are thus part of community relations and street life. During campaigns, candidates organize colorful mass rallies in stadiums. These are always occasions for music and dancing. Campaign theme songs are sung, often by youth groups and women's choirs, and new dances are performed to warm up the audience ahead of the politicians' speeches.

Political parties also organize smaller-scale neighborhood gatherings. Rented tents, chairs, and a sound system are set up in a street, often in front of the house of an important community leader backing the politician. Speeches interspersed with interludes of singing and dancing begin in the afternoon and continue until dinner time. Griots who back the politician recite anecdotes. The women of the community are particularly visible during such occasions. They are expected to grace the event by wearing their finest dresses and newest hairdos.

ALCOHOL AND TOBACCO

The consumption of alcohol and tobacco is generally condemned by Muslim religious authorities. These drugs are prohibited in Sufi shrine towns and in neighborhoods under their control. Yet Senegal is a secular state where these products are authorized for sale. Indeed, as elsewhere, the government levies a sin tax on both.

Dakar breweries produce beer, but all other alcoholic beverages are imported. Alcohol is served in upscale restaurants and most hotels. Bars can be found in the downtowns of every city except those run by the Sufis, and alcohol can be purchased at a select number of licensed general stores. Yet the consumption of alcohol is by no means socially acceptable. Alcohol must never enter a Muslim house. Public displays of drunkenness bring shame to the family and cause a scandal in the neighborhood. At best, drinking is tolerated as long as it remains discrete, out of the public eye.

Smoking is also subject to social opprobrium. The Tijaniyya, Mouride, and Layène orders prohibit their members from smoking and expressly prohibit tobacco in towns and neighborhoods under their control. Only the Qadiri order permits it. As with alcohol, smoking cigarettes is tolerated as long as it is discrete. Women, especially those from families with conservative religious values, cannot be seen smoking in public.

8

Music, Dance, and Sports

MUSIC AND DANCE are the most developed of all the art forms expressive of Senegalese culture. They are essential to any definition of tradition. They are lived, almost daily, as personal forms of expression. And they thrive within the mass-meditated, global pop cultural environment.

TRADITIONAL MUSIC

All of Senegal's traditional cultures, distinguished by ethnicity (Wolof, Sereer, Halpulaar, Mandinka, Diola, and so forth), express themselves through a combination of orature (poetry, narratives to music) and dancing supported by music-making. Most of the music-making, as most of the orature, fell to the griot caste, and both they and their traditions continue to infuse music today.

Traditional music-making employs a number of string and percussion instruments. The most important of these is a plucked lute, called the *xalam* in Wolof. There are several varieties, but most have five strings. The resonators are of wood with stretched skin surfaces. It is the *xalam* that provides the melody, or "voice" of the song. The *xalam* is played as far north as Morocco, where it is called the *gimbri*. A smaller, single string bowed lute, called the *riti,* is used for some griot songs. In Mandika culture it is the *kora* harp-lute that serves this purpose. The *kora* can have up to 21 strings. It used to be used only in the Casamance, but with Malian music becoming more popular worldwide, it is increasingly being used for traditional music in Wolof, as this is what visiting tourists expect. The principal percussion instrument is the small *tama* drum. Made of wood, the *tama* has an hourglass shape. Tension on the skin striking surfaces at each end is procured from a mesh of bracing ropes. The drum is played in the armpit. The pressure exerted on the ropes by the arm of the player determines the tone of the skin, which is struck with a short stick. Because of the great variety of tones produced by the *tama,* it is often called the "talking drum." The *tama* player can effectively reproduce sequential tones similar to those of the human voice. A variety of other drum types, large and small, are used to produce rhythm. The *sabar* is worn at the hip, suspended from the shoulder on a strap. It is the favored instrument of women's dance parties, the *tànn-béer.* The *jembe,* of Mandinka origin, is played between the knees. It has recently become popular because of the global success of Malian music. All these instruments are manufactured either by the griots themselves or by member of the *lawbe* (woodworkers) caste. There are no traditional wind instruments, such as flutes.

There are three traditional types of music. First are the solo works, where a griot plucks a *xalam* or bows a *riti* to accompany his narrative. Women griots never play instruments; they always sing to the accompaniment of male musicians. Second are performances by groups, orchestras, and bands. Both strings and percussion are used to accompany the singer, who is also a griot. The third type consists of percussion bands, drummers who produce music specifically for dancing. Historically, whether performed publicly or in private, each type of music had a specific place in the lives of individuals and communities. There was hardly a family or community event—be it a wedding, a baptism, a celebration of circumcisions, farming, warfare, homage to the king—that was not accompanied by some form of music, recitation, and dance.

This heritage is still a living tradition today. As in the past, at street level, singing, dancing, and drumming continue to enrich family life and community events. Moreover, artists of griot origin dominate much contemporary musical production. All of Senegal's top female vocalists—Fatou Gewel, Kiné Lam, and Ndèye Mbaye—are griots. They sing praise songs to the accompaniment of male backup vocalists, dancers, and drummers. For the most part, praise songs are religious in character and involve the founding figures of Senegalese Sufism, such as Sheikh Ahmadou Bamba Mbacké and Al Hajj Malick Sy, or their sons, the caliphs of the orders, who are adored.

The drumming tradition has done well under modern pop conditions. The first to perfect the pop genre was Doudou Ndiaye Rose (b. 1928). Of griot origin, Doudou Ndiaye Rose was a member of the National Ballet in Dakar before leaving to lead a host of drum bands in the 1970s. The bands explored the country's regionally and ethnically specific drumming repertoire. In the early 1980s his daughters joined the band, which was a first because women had never drummed in public before. Today, even some of Doudou Ndiaye Rose's granddaughters drum in his band.

TRANSATLANTIC CONNECTIONS: BLUES AND JAZZ

The traditional instruments and musical genres described earlier were the basis for the evolution of Senegalese music during the twentieth century. This evolution has been marked by two developments: the influence of various African American and Latin American genres, and the growth of mass-mediated pop music. Every major twentieth-century African American musical genre, from blues to rap, has impacted Senegal's music output. In some ways, this is a form of "roots coming home," meaning that African American music is itself rooted in African music, and the transatlantic connection functions both ways.

Blues is the oldest and deepest of the transatlantic genres. Vocal melisma, wavy intonations, and soulfulness bind American blues singing to the West African griot tradition. Some consider the Senegambian plucked *xalam* to be the ancestor of the American plucked banjo. Whatever the case, when recordings of American blues singers were first heard in Senegal, people intuitively got the gist of the songs even though they could not understand the English lyrics.

Of all American music genres, it is jazz that exerted a determining influence on emerging Senegalese pop. Recordings of Afro-Cuban jazz, called rumba, began to be played on Senegalese radio in the 1930s, and the genre immediately became popular in the cities. American GIs passing through Saint Louis and Dakar with their instruments during World War II brought new strains of jazz to the nightlife. The main novelty of jazz for the Senegalese musical tradition was the introduction of brass wind instruments such as the trumpet, trombone, and saxophone.

Jazz was embraced by Senegal's emerging urban middle class, which saw it as an antidote to official French colonial culture. By the 1950s jazz bands in Saint Louis, singing in Spanish, were producing their own versions of Cuban hits, while Dakar's neighborhood dance clubs served as venues for local orchestras. Senegal's jazz era is best represented by Aminata Fall (1942–2002). She became enthralled with jazz when, as a child selling peanuts in the streets of Saint Louis, she heard the voices of Mahalia Jackson and other American singers coming from a theater. By 1958 she had become lead singer for Star Jazz, Saint Louis's top jazz orchestra. Later, she added gospel and blues to her repertoire. Likewise, calypso, rhythm and blues, and soul were integrated, in

turn, to the local repertoires of Senegal's jazz bands. Though Senegalese pop
music has moved in new directions, jazz remains an important genre to this
day. An international jazz festival was held in Dakar in 1980, and since 1992,
Saint Louis has held an annual international jazz festival.

Afro-Cuban–type jazz remained the undisputed rhythm of urban dance
clubs until the 1970s, and it is still associated with the independence generation. Dance music diversified somewhat in the mid-1970s when reggae and
Zairian *soukous* became the rage. Reggae, with its message of African struggle
and liberation, was immediately popular with the youth, but the music had
little resonance with Senegalese musicians. *Soukous,* on the other hand, was
an exhilarating dance genre produced with traditional Zairian instruments,
which were not so different from Senegalese instruments, along with guitars
and horns. Meanwhile, the Afro-Cuban sound was being fused with traditional Senegalese dance rhythms by bands such as Dakar's Orchestre Baobab.

MBALAX AND YELE

In the 1970s, Dakar's dance bands began fusing the horns and guitars of
jazz and rock with traditional drum rhythms. The result was a hybrid urban
sound called *mbalax. Mbalax* is characterized by ferocious, syncopated *sabar*
drumming, designed to keep women dancing for hours, and "vocals" provided by the *tama* talking drum. The 1980s witnessed the rise and triumph
of *mbalax* over the entire Senegalese pop and dance scene.

The greatest master of urban *mbalax* has been Youssou N'Dour (b. 1959).
Youssou grew up in Dakar's Médina neighborhood. Though his mother had
been a celebrated griot before marrying his father, Youssou's musical education was steeped in the capital's brassy rumba bands rather than in family
tradition. At 14 he was singing in Diamono, one of Dakar's top bands,
and was frequently invited to perform at the Miami, the nightclub at the
heart of musical innovation at the time. His first big hit with Diamono
was "Xalis" (Money), recorded in 1979. It made him a star in France as
well as in Senegal. In subsequent years he progressively reduced the horns
and keyboard and brought the *tama* and *sabar* drums to the fore. Youssou
N'Dour's purging of rumba elements from *mbalax* helped position it as the
music of the postindependence generation. N'Dour's lyrics spoke directly to
their experiences with relationships, family, and money, and they did so in
an urban, street idiom quite distinct from the "deep" Wolof of traditional
griot orature.

While not exactly a politicized form of music, *mbalax* nonetheless became
the music of the *sopi* (meaning "change") generation: the unemployed, disenfranchised young people of the 1980s who backed the opposition parties'

calls for change. Street culture, and dancing especially, was their principal outlet, and the sound was *mbalax*. Throughout the early 1980s, official culture, the culture of their parents' generation, refused to acknowledge the new sound. Government radio and TV stations, the only ones to broadcast in Senegal, played only traditional griot songs and traditional drumming. *Mbalax* was deemed too vulgar. Senegal's youth had to tune in to Radio Gambia to hear it. However, things changed following the February 1988 elections. On election night a state of emergency was declared in Dakar. Youth took to the streets chanting "sopi." President Diouf's government realized that it could no longer afford to alienate a generation that would soon represent a substantial proportion of the electorate. It therefore reversed its attitude toward *mbalax,* allowing it on radio and lending its support to live performances.

Mbalax was hegemonic in the 1990s. It was played and heard everywhere. It diversified too; there were fusion forms such as *rock-mbalax* and *zouk-mbalax*. Also, traditional dance rhythms from across the country were systematically reinterpreted and electrified to produce one *mbalax* hit after another. Youssou N'Dour was now an international superstar, performing around the world with the likes of Peter Gabriel, Sting, and Stevie Wonder. Other singers also rose to the top of the pop charts. Ismael Lô (b. 1956) first studied art in Dakar before joining Super Diamono, one of the successor jazz and blues bands to Diamono, in 1979. In 1984 he embarked on a solo singing career. Ismael Lô's style is more folk than dance. His preferred instruments are the harmonica and the acoustic guitar. His soulful signature 1988 hit "Taajabóon" set the tone for a slew of subsequent internationally released recordings.

Baaba Maal (b. 1953) also rose to greatness on an *mbalax* foundation. Born into the fisherman caste of the Futa Toro, Baaba Maal broke with family tradition by becoming a singer and musician. Along with guitarist Mansour Seck, Baaba Maal first recorded *Djaam Leelii* in 1984. This acoustic recording of traditional ballads is now considered classic *yele*. Baaba Maal then created a band called Daande Leñol (Voice of the Race, in Pulaar), which has produced a steady string of hit electric recordings, beginning with "Wango" (1988), a song about the caste system that he had breached. Baaba Maal considers himself the cultural ambassador of the Futa Toro and the voice of the Halpulaaren. His electric music has explored the Futa's dance traditions, *yele* in particular, and fused them with reggae, soul, and hip-hop. Yet he also continues to record beautiful tradition-inspired acoustic music like *Baayo* (1991). Mostly, though, it is his extraordinary voice, strong and piercing enough to soar well above the tumult of the *tama,* that has propelled him to international stardom.

RAP

By the mid-1990s the social context and significance of *mbalax* had changed. The music of disenfranchised urban youth in the 1980s and the music of the Set Setal movement of 1990 had become a ubiquitous, mass-meditated, mesmerizing, mindless pop promoting consumerism. The same music that the sole, government-owned radio station had refused to play had now become associated with every fleeting fashion in clothing, hairstyle, jewelry, cosmetics, and cell phones, and was used in TV ads to market everything from fruit drinks to construction materials.

This was the context in which hip-hop and rap emerged. Senegalese rap, while embracing the American rap aesthetic, is far more akin to French rap in terms of content. The lyrics are highly politicized, and Senegalese rappers consider themselves "edutainers," that is, popular educators as well as entertainers. They rap directly and openly about drugs, sex, poverty, school, and authority, as well as international and global issues such as Sierra Leone's conflict diamonds, human rights, and paternalistic Western attitudes toward Africa. Senegalese rappers especially eschew the violence they see as characteristic of U.S. rap.

American hip-hop and rap acquired a following among Dakar youth in the late 1980s, but it took a concert by Franco-Chadian rap superstar MC Solar in 1992 to launch the local rap scene. The first Senegalese rap group to achieve success was PBS (Positive Black Soul). As their name suggests, PBS aim to promote "positivity" in response to daily problems. They rap about maintaining a healthy body and getting an education. The title of their first recording, *Bul Faale* (1994), came to designate an entire post-*mbalax* generation. *Bul faale* can be politely translated as "so what," or "who cares," though less polite translations are also possible. The term came to designate the twenty-something generation whose lack of resources left it outside the *mbalax*-induced consumerism. Members of this urban culture confronted older generations by overtly contravening conservative values. They exhibited their bodies in sexual ways, refused to speak proper French, mixed American English with their Wolof, mixed erotic dancing with their Islam, and became the greatest fans of traditional wrestling, a sport considered vulgar and un-Islamic. And they did all this to the sound of rap music. Though President Diouf tried to co-opt the self-styled "New Generation Bul Faale" by publicly welcoming PBS home after their hugely successful African tour in 1997, the *Bul Faale* generation massively supported Abdoulaye Wade and the PDS during the 2000 elections.

Although in recent years the *Bul Faale* phenomenon seems to have played itself out, rap has not. Akon, a Senegalese American rapper, has had great success on both sides of the Atlantic in recent years. Rap remains the most political form of music produced and performed in Senegal today. An all-female group—female rappers take names beginning with "Sister" and "Lady"—called Alif (Attaque Libératoire de l'Infanterie Féministe) combines rap with *sabar* rhythms and raps about things like incest and the exploitation of rural girls as housemaids by Dakar's bourgeoisie.

Dakar is the rap capital. Large-scale concerts that bring together Senegalese, American, and French rappers are frequently organized. Moreover, there are currently more than 3,000 active crews (rap groups call themselves "crews") in the Dakar area. As with so many other cultural expressions in Senegal, rap is lived at street level. Neighborhoods have rival crews that compete for top honors in nightclubs. If *mbalax* is the sound of the Médina neighborhood, rap is the sound of the distant, impoverished, "irregular" suburbs of Pikine, Thiaroye, and Guediawaye.

SPORTS: WRESTLING AND FOOTBALL

Sports are an important form of cultural expression. While some sports, like traditional wrestling, are rooted in Senegal's ancient rural civilization, they are also a dynamic part of contemporary urban and national culture.

Like traditional wrestling forms elsewhere in the world, Senegalese wrestling began as a martial art. It was a highly coded sport closely linked to warfare; in fact, it can be categorized as a form of war for peacetime. The coding of the sport was closely linked to traditional religious rites and depended on relations to local spirits in particular. Because of its dependence on traditional religion, traditional wrestling has continued only among the most recently Islamized or the non-Islamized groups in the country. It is practiced by the Diola, the Sereer, and the Lebu, but it has completely disappeared from the Wolof heartland and from the Futa Toro.

Wrestling, in its traditional village context, is practiced only by young men, men who are circumcised but not yet married. Though it certainly is a physical act, it is experienced as a psychic confrontation. A wrestling match pits the psyches of the protagonists against each other. Each of these psyches is aided, or not, by the protective spirits of its respective community. Wrestlers must thus prepare mentally as well as physically before each match, just as warriors did before each battle. The backing of communal spirits is gained by visiting shrines and making offerings. Libations are made. A multitude of specially confected talismans and charms of various kinds are then attached to the body.

The traditional wrestling matches, called *mbapat,* are carefully orchestrated affairs. The *mbapat* takes place on the village's central public square and is very much a public event. The date is set by tradition; often it marks the end of harvest season. Teams are organized by neighborhood within a village, or else teams from different villages are arrayed against each other. Individual wrestlers from opposing teams are pitted against each other in a series of short matches. Each match begins with special dances. Accompanied by drummers and supporters, the wrestlers show off their bodies and challenge each other. Griots are present to extol the attributes of the wrestlers. The rules are quite simple. A wrestler must "throw" the opponent without being "thrown" himself. Only the feet and hands may touch the ground. No part of the torso, the back, the forearms, or the calves of the leg may touch the ground. More than a test of strength and agility, a wrestler gets thrown when his protective spiritual support system is breached by the opponent. Once the wrestlers begin, matches rarely last more than a few minutes each.

Traditional wrestling matches usually take place in the afternoon and end with music and dancing in the evening. While only young men may wrestle, the matches attract many people, especially young women, as spectators. There is no doubt that the spectacular display of the male body, and of individual courage and prowess, are essential to the show. This traditional form of wrestling is still practiced in Sereer and Diola villages. The most important matches today are the Xulam festival in Oussouye (lower Casamance) and the Fatick wrestling weekend.

Traditional, rural-based wrestling has taken hold in cities, and in Dakar in particular. Starting in the 1920s, various neighborhoods of the capital, principally those with a large Lebu population, began challenging each other to matches. The city's showbiz impresarios rented movie theaters for these events. In the 1930s and 1940s special arenas were created and full-fledged competitions for titles were held. By that time European boxing techniques had been fused with the traditional wrestling techniques. In the 1950s, in the lead-up to independence, politicians began patronizing urban wrestling matches. Wrestling was declared Senegal's official national sport in 1959. Its rules and regulations were institutionalized and national leagues and federations were put into place.

Since independence, traditional wrestling has remained a very popular sport. Every generation has had its stars and heroes, its memorable fights, and its share of scandals (match fixing, political meddling, nepotism, and corruption). Yet, despite its great popularity, official status, and high rewards, the sport remained tainted by its rural roots and traditional spiritual mystique. Senegal's Muslim clerics condemned it as un-Islamic and detrimental to the proper education of young people, while the Western-educated elite considered it vulgar. It is perhaps no accident, then, that the irreverent *Bul Faale* generation took to the sport so wholeheartedly in the 1990s.

Consequent to the increased visibility and "coolness" of the *Bul Faale,* traditional wrestling has been reborn. It is awarded extensive coverage in the media, particularly in the print press. Major competitions, often held in the city's biggest stadiums on public holidays, are televised. Wrestling has always been theatrical in its combination of sport, music, dance, and showy display, but it has now become part of show business. Star heavyweight champions take on frightful names like "Tyson," "Muhammad Ali," "Saddam," and "Bombardier." They have huge followings, and their careers are closely chronicled in the tabloid press. They are TV personalities. Pop songs are composed for them. Like sports stars everywhere, they are solicited by corporations to sponsor products. One wrestler, Mustapha Guèye, ran (unsuccessfully) for municipal office in 1996. Another, Tyson (the darling of the *Bul Faale,* who likes to parade around the stadium draped in the U.S. flag), offered very public support to President Diouf in his bid for reelection in 2000.

Mostly, though, professional wrestlers put on a great show. They show up in the arena or stadium surrounded by a loud retinue of trainers, spiritual guides, drummers, and dancers. Their impressive bodies, bedecked in talismans, are flexed and then offered up to libations of magic dust or secret liquid concoctions. The dances, always new and different, which they perform to challenge opponents, are met with howls and screams of delight from their supporters, both male and female, in the stands. Meanwhile, seasoned sports reporters and expert analysts comment on their every move for the television audience.

Unrelated to its wrestling tradition, Senegal had a fleeting moment of glory in world championship boxing with Battling Siki (1897–1925). Battling Siki was born Amadou Mbarick Fall in Saint Louis. He moved to Paris as a youth and took up boxing as a career shortly before World War I. He emerged from that war a decorated hero and went on to fight his way to the top as light heavyweight. He defeated the world champion, Georges Carpentier, in 1922. The first black world champion, he was hailed a hero not only among Africans but among African Americans as well. Following his victory, Siki swore he would take on the reigning world heavyweight champion, Jack Dempsey, but that fight never happened. Not very disciplined in his training, Siki took to the Parisian nightlife, becoming a demimonde fixture on its boulevards. In 1923 he lost his title to Irishman Mike McTigue in Dublin and then lost another important fight to American Kid Norfolk in New York City. He remained in New York, where he settled into a life of drink and barroom brawling. He was found shot dead in a street in 1925.

Senegal's most popular sport after wrestling is football (American soccer). Football has no equivalent in traditional culture. Rather, Senegalese football is a product of colonial influence and remains closely linked to the development of that sport in France. Moreover, Senegal's football culture is nourished by the global football culture.

Senegalese football has two different layers. There are the official premier and minor leagues, organized on a professional basis, and there are the *nawetaan* clubs, organized by local associations. The official leagues set up shortly after independence suffer from low salaries and chronic underinvestment in infrastructure. They have, however, been very successful stepping stones for lucrative international careers. Many of Senegal's top players— El-Hadji Diouf, Henri Camara, Souleymane Diawara, Mamadou Niang, and Guirane Ndaw—play for French or English premier league teams. They are household names in Senegal, which, like Brazil, is a world-class exporter of professional football players. The football relationship between France and its former colony was rocked during the 2002 World Cup. The opening match of that competition pitted France, the defending world champion, against Senegal. To the astonishment of nearly everyone, Senegal defeated France and went on to the semifinals.

The local *nawetaan* clubs constitute the vital, beating heart of Senegalese football. The term *nawetaan* was first used in the early twentieth century to designate the migrant agricultural laborers who traveled the Peanut Basin during the rainy season. As in their home villages, these young men created their own associations to maintain good cheer in difficult situations and to protect their interests whenever possible. One of their favorite activities was the organization of football matches. In the 1960s, due partly to rural-urban migration, *nawetaan* football clubs began to appear in Senegalese cities, and in Dakar's various neighborhoods in particular. Today, over 2,000 of these local clubs, distributed across the country, account for most of Senegal's football activity. While more or less officially sanctioned, they rely almost entirely on local resources—merchants, shopkeepers, small and medium-sized businesses, and so forth—to donate uniforms, trophies, and small cash prizes. The *nawetaan* clubs are yet another example of Senegal's thriving street culture and the important role that local grassroots organizations play in public life.

Bibliography

Babou, Cheikh Anta. *Fighting the Greater Jihad: Amadu Bamba and the Founding of the Muridiyya of Senegal, 1853–1913.* Athens: Ohio University Press, 2007.

Balonze, John (ed.). *Street Children in Senegal.* Translated by Shannon Delaney. Paris: GYAN/Editions GEM, 2006.

Baum, Robert M. *Shrines of the Slave Trade: Diola Religion and Society in Precolonial Senegambia.* Oxford: Oxford University Press, 1999.

Boone, Catherine. *Merchant Capital and the Roots of State Power in Senegal, 1930–1985.* Cambridge: Cambridge University Press, 1992.

Bourdier, Jean-Paul and Trinh T. Minh-Ha. *Drawn from African Dwellings.* Bloomington: Indiana University Press, 1996.

Brooks, George E. *Eurafricans in Western Africa: Commerce, Social Status, Gender, and Religious Observance from the Sixteenth to the Eighteenth Century.* Athens: Ohio University Press (Western African Studies) and Oxford: James Currey, 2003.

Castaldi, Francesca. *Choreographies of African Identities: Négritude, Dance, and the National Ballet of Senegal.* Urbana: University of Illinois Press, 2006.

Clark, Andrew F. *From Frontier to Backwater: Economy and Society in the Upper Senegal Valley 1850–1920.* Lanham, MD: University Press of America, 1999.

Colvin, Lucie Gallistel. *Historical Dictionary of Senegal.* London: Scarecrow Press, 1981.

Dilley, Roy M. *Islamic and Caste Knowledge Practices among Haalpulaar'en in Senegal: Between Mosque and Termite Mound.* Edinburgh, Scotland: Edinburgh University Press, 2004.

Gadjigo, Samba, and Ralph Faulkingham. *Ousmane Sembene: Dialogues with Critics and Writers.* Amherst: University of Massachusetts Press, 1993.

Galvan, Dennis C. *The State Must Be Our Master of Fire: How Peasants Craft Culturally Sustainable Development in Senegal.* Berkeley: University of California Press, 2004.

Gellar, Sheldon. *Democracy in Senegal: Tocquevillian Analytics in Africa.* New York: Palgrave Macmillan, 2005.

Glover, John. *Sufism and Jihad in Modern Senegal: The Murid Order.* Rochester, NY: University of Rochester Press, 2007.

Gomez, Michael A. *Pragmatism in the Age of Jihad: The Precolonial State of Bundu.* Cambridge: Cambridge University Press, 1992.

Hale, Thomas A. *Griots and Griottes: Masters of Words and Music.* Bloomington: Indiana University Press, 1999.

Harney, Elizabeth. *In Senghor's Shadow: Art, Politics, and the Avant-Garde in Senegal, 1960–1995.* Durham, NC: Duke University Press, 2004.

Hecht, David, and Maliqalim Simon. *Invisible Governance: The Art of African Micropolitics.* Brooklyn, NY: Autonomedia, 1994.

Johnson, G. Wesley. *The Emergence of Black Politics in Senegal: The Struggle for Power in the Four Communes, 1900–1920.* Stanford, CA: Stanford University Press, 1971.

Kesteloot, Lilyan. *Black Writers in French: A Literary History of Negritude.* Washington, DC: Howard University Press, 1991.

Klein, Martin. *Slavery and Colonial Rule in French West Africa.* Cambridge: Cambridge University Press, 1998.

Lewis Renaud, Michelle. *Women at the Crossroads: A Prostitute Community's Response to AIDS in Urban Senegal.* New York: Routledge, 1997.

Mark, Peter. *"Portuguese" Style and Luso-African Identity: Precolonial Senegambia, Sixteenth–Nineteenth Centuries.* Bloomington: Indiana University Press, 2002.

Mbacké, Khadim. *Sufism and Religious Brotherhoods in Senegal.* Translated by Eric Ross and edited by John Hunwick. Princeton, NJ: Marcus Wiener Publishers, 2005.

McDonald Shaw, Thomas. *The Fulani Matrix of Beauty and Art in the Djolof Region of Senegal.* New York: Edwin Mellen Press, 1993.

Petty, Sheila. *A Call to Action: The Films of Ousmane Sembene.* Westport, CT: Praeger, 1996.

Roberts, Allen A., and Mary Nooter Roberts. *A Saint in the City: Sufi Arts of Urban Senegal.* Los Angeles: University of California Press, 2003.

Robinson, David. *Paths of Accommodation: Muslim Societies and French Colonial Authorities in Senegal and Mauritania, 1880–1920.* Athens, OH: Ohio University Press, 2000.

Ross, Eric. *Sufi City: Urban Design and Archetypes in Touba.* Rochester, NY: University of Rochester Press, 2006.

Sanneh, Lamine. *The Jakhanke Muslim Clerics: A Religious and Historical Study of Islam in Senegambia.* New York: University Press of America, 1989.

Searing, James F. *"God Alone Is King": Islam and Emancipation in Senegal, the Wolof Kingdoms of Kajoor and Bawol, 1859–1914.* London: Heinemann/James Currey/David Philip Publishers, 2002.

———. *West African Slavery and Atlantic Commerce: The Senegal River Valley, 1700–1860.* Cambridge: Cambridge University Press, 2003.

Shaw, Thomas. *Irony and Illusion in the Architecture of Imperial Dakar.* New York: Mellen Press, 2006.

Villalon, Leonardo A. *Islamic Society and State Power in Senegal: Disciples and Citizens in Fatick.* Cambridge: Cambridge University Press, 1995.

Index

Wolofal, 13, 44, 54

Women, 1, 11, 17, 20, 32, 34, 37, 42, 46–48, 50, 52, 65, 69–71, 74–79, 81–84, 86–90, 93, 99, 102, 105–6, 108–10, 114

World War I, 21–22, 66, 115

World War II, 7, 21, 23, 25–26, 46, 63, 67, 109

Wrestling, 2, 47, 100, 105, 112–15

Xalam lute, 8, 107–9

Youth, 8, 24, 29–30, 47, 54, 79, 82, 84–85, 90–93, 102, 105, 110–12

Zâwiyas, 67, 102–3

Ziguinchor, 10, 38, 50, 100, 105

About the Author

ERIC S. ROSS is Associate Professor of Geography at the School of Humanities and Social Sciences, Al Akhawayn University in Ifrane, Morocco.